The Water Cycle

SCIENCE FOUNDATIONS

SCIENCE FOUNDATIONS

The Water Cycle

NIKOLE BROOKS BETHEA, PE

CHELSEA HOUSE
An Infobase Learning Company

Science Foundations: The Water Cycle
Copyright © 2011 by Infobase Learning

Chelsea House
An imprint of Infobase Learning
132 West 31st Street
New York, NY 10001

Library of Congress Cataloging-in-Publication Data
Bethea, Nikole Brooks.
  The water cycle / Nikole Brooks Bethea.
      p. cm. — (Science foundations)
  Includes bibliographical references and index.
  ISBN 978-1-60413-943-3 (hardcover)
  1. Hydrologic cycle—Juvenile literature. I. Title. II. Series: Science foundations
(Chelsea House Publishers)
  GB848.B48 2011
  551.48—dc22
                                  2010047646

Chelsea House books are available at special discounts when purchased in bulk quantities for businesses, associations, institutions, or sales promotions. Please call our Special Sales Department in New York at (212) 967-8800 or (800) 322-8755.

You can find Chelsea House on the World Wide Web at
http://www.infobaselearning.com

Text design by Kerry Casey
Cover design by Alicia Post
Composition by EJB Publishing Services
Cover printed by Yurchak Printing, Landisville, Pa.
Book printed and bound by Yurchak Printing, Landisville, Pa.
Date printed: September 2011
Printed in the United States of America

10 9 8 7 6 5 4 3 2 1

This book is printed on acid-free paper.

All links and Web addresses were checked and verified to be correct at the time of publication. Because of the dynamic nature of the Web, some addresses and links may have changed since publication and may no longer be valid.

Contents

Historical Understanding of the Water Cycle

Scientists believe that Earth is 4.6 billion years old. Water has been on the planet for at least the last 3.8 billion years. During this time, Earth's water has been in constant movement.

The **water cycle** is the continuous movement of water on, above, and under Earth's surface. Water moves from the oceans to the atmosphere through **evaporation**, the process by which water changes from a liquid to a gas. Water moves back to the land surface through rain and snow; it then soaks into the ground or flows into streams and rivers. Eventually, water makes its way back into the ocean where the cycle starts again. During its journey, water changes states between solid (ice), liquid (water), and gas (water vapor). The water cycle is more formally called the **hydrologic cycle**.

ANCIENT GREEK VIEWS

The ancient Greeks recorded some of the first theories about water. They believed that nature was understandable. Many Greek philosophers at that time attempted to explain the natural world through reason and logic; they did not rely on religious or mythical explanations to develop their philosophies.

The Greeks believed that water was one of the four elements forming the universe. The other three were fire, air, and earth. These four basic elements are not the same elements of today's chemistry, such as hydrogen or helium; instead, they were principles. Fire was combustion, not the actual flame. Air was whatever existed directly above Earth and could include **clouds** or **fog**. (Today, clouds are known to be masses of tiny water drops floating in the atmosphere; fog is simply a cloud resting on the ground.) Water was the principle of fluid flow, and earth represented solids. To the ancient Greeks, different proportions of water, fire, air, and earth explained differences in materials.

Ancient Greeks generally understood that water evaporated to form rain. Many of their writings established the idea that the Sun draws up, or raises, water from the sea, and this water falls again as rain. Although they had a basic understanding of rain, the source of water flowing in rivers and **springs**—places where water flows naturally from the ground to the surface—was a popular topic of Greek philosophy that was not well understood.

The earlier Greek philosophers believed that an underground ocean fed rivers, streams, and springs. Thales (624–548 B.C.) is often considered to be the first Greek natural philosopher. Thales believed water was the original source of everything, including earth, and that planet Earth rested, or floated, on water. He believed that water held up Earth the same way that it supports a piece of floating wood. In this idea, salt is filtered out as the water flows up to Earth's surface to supply rivers, springs, and streams.

A competing idea on the source of rivers, streams, and springs was that they formed from rainfall. Anaxagoras (500–428 B.C.) believed that Earth was hollow and was filled with water and that both rain and the water within Earth formed rivers. The well-known Greek philosopher Plato (427–348 B.C.) often wrote imaginary conversations between people. Although this style sometimes makes determining which of his writings are actually fact and which are fiction difficult, Plato did offer two ideas about how rivers and springs formed. His first view was that water from the ocean flowed in underground channels that rose to the surface. His second view was that the soil absorbed rainfall as if it were a natural water pot. This absorbed water was the source of rivers and springs.

Figure 1.1   Greek philosopher Aristotle was one of the most popular figures in the development of Western philosophy. His views on science shaped ancient Greek scholarship and city building.

The idea that rainfall was the source of rivers was apparently popular enough to warrant an attack from the Greek philosopher Aristotle (384–322 B.C.). Aristotle lived in a dry region and did not think that it rained enough to supply rivers. He thought that, like sponges, the mountains soaked up air and changed it into the water that formed rivers. He argued that a large amount of water constantly flowed each day in rivers; therefore, the size of the underground reservoir required to store water for a year's worth of flow would be as large as Earth.

Although the ancient Greeks did not understand the water cycle as it is understood today, progress was made during that time. Greek society began to question the natural world and search for answers.

After 300 B.C., Greek civilization declined. By 100 B.C., Rome was the center of culture.

ANCIENT ROMAN VIEWS

The early Romans were widely known as being practical engineers. They constructed great **aqueducts** (channels that carry water)

Aristotle's Lasting Influence

Aristotle (384–322 B.C.) was arguably the most influential of the ancient Greek philosophers. He was a student of Plato at the Academy in Athens, Greece, and later became a teacher there. After Plato died, Aristotle left the Academy to tutor Prince Alexander (the Great) for seven years. When he returned to Athens, he established his own school, the Lyceum. Much of what we know about Aristotle's philosophies comes from his lecture notes at the Lyceum.

Aristotle wrote *Meteoroligica*, a collection of books that includes his ideas on meteorology, astronomy, chemistry, geology, and physics. These books may not necessarily give accurate descriptions of processes in the water cycle, but they are important because some of Aristotle's ideas influenced thought and philosophy for close to 2,000 years.

Aristotle believed in the four "Earthly" elements—fire, air, water, and earth. He also believed that hot, cold, dry, or wet conditions would cause one element to change to another element. For example, Aristotle thought that coldness changed the air surrounding Earth into water.

and sewage systems. However, they offered few new ideas on the water cycle.

Marcus Vitruvius (90–20 B.C.) was a Roman architect and a military engineer under Julius Caesar. He wrote *De Architectura*, which included 10 books on architecture. In these, he included some practical suggestions for finding **groundwater**. One of these examples required a person to lie on his stomach before sunrise, placing his chin on the ground to look for rising vapors. Vitruvius also provided a table of soil types, which included the amount and taste of groundwater that one could expect from each soil type. He noted that a large amount of rainfall occurs in the valleys between mountains and that snow remains there longer because of dense forests. He also observed that melted snow from the mountains seeped into the soil, producing springs in the valleys below. Interestingly, this last idea is correct, although it was not widely accepted at the time.

Consequently, it fell as rain. In the same way, he thought air passed through Earth's crust. Cold conditions beneath Earth's surface changed the air into water. He believed this newly formed water supplied river flow.

Aristotle rejected the belief that wind is air in motion. Instead, he claimed that there were two types of evaporation: moist and dry. The philosopher noted that *moist evaporation* occurred when the Sun drew water upward, and *dry evaporation* occurred when the Sun warmed and dried Earth itself. He believed that moist evaporation caused rain, whereas dry evaporation caused wind.

In the thirteenth century A.D., Aristotle's works were translated into Latin. Before this time, Western Europe indirectly knew his works through Roman encyclopedias. Western Europe was directly reintroduced to Aristotle's ideas when his works were translated into Latin. Because he did not base his ideas on scientific experimentation, many of them were erroneous and therefore hindered scientific progress. One example is the reappearance of his idea that wind was not moving air. Like many of his other ideas, most people were afraid to challenge it because Aristotle was so well respected.

Figure 1.2 This restored section of one of the longest aqueducts built in the Roman Empire is located in Oudna, Tunisia. An enclosed water channel is visible at the top. Constructed during the late first to early second century A.D., this aqueduct carried 8.5 million gallons (32 million liters) of water per day from its source at Mount Zaghouan to the city of Carthage, near modern-day Tunis.

Lucius Annaeus Seneca (4 B.C.–A.D. 65), a teacher of Emperor Nero, opposed the idea that rainwater seeped into the ground to form groundwater. He claimed that the rainfall was never heavy enough to wet the soil in his vineyard to more than 10 feet (3 meters) deep. In his book *Natural Questions*, Seneca summarized ideas about the source of river flow, including that (1) moisture inside Earth was forced out at its surface, (2) darkness and cold inside Earth changed air into water, and (3) earth was converted to water.

The main contribution of the ancient Romans was the collection of Greek knowledge into handbooks and encyclopedias. Gaius

Plinius Secundus, often called "Pliny the Elder" (A.D. 23–79), offered no original theories; however, he did gather prior Greek philosophies into huge encyclopedias.

The Roman Empire fell in the fifth century A.D. Their collections of Greek ideas allowed the information to be passed along to the Middle Ages. If the Romans had not collected this information and passed it along, many of the Greek ideas would possibly have been lost.

MIDDLE AGES AND THE RENAISSANCE

The Middle Ages spanned 1,000 years following the fall of the Roman Empire. Surprisingly, little scientific advancement was made during this time. For this reason, this time period is often called the Dark Ages. The Church had become powerful and did not encourage the investigation of nature. Knowledge was viewed as useful only if it explained the scriptures. Much of the scientific writing from the Middle Ages simply reinterprets earlier Greek thought in religious terms. In the fourteenth century, the Renaissance brought about a revived interest in scientific learning.

Leonardo Da Vinci (1452–1519), the great painter of the *Mona Lisa,* was also a military engineer, architect, and scientist. Da Vinci described how heat caused water vapor to rise to higher elevations where it condensed. The water then fell again as rain. Da Vinci had an accurate understanding of this portion of the water cycle; however, he lacked an understanding of the source of rivers and other flowing waters. He explained that heat drew seawater up through veins in mountains where it flowed out through cracks to create rivers. He thought that this process occurred in much the same way that the body raises blood to its head where the blood can flow out through cuts. Da Vinci thought that there were similarities between river flow on Earth's surface and the body's circulatory system. He compared oceans and **tides** with blood and lungs.

Bernard Palissy (1510–1589), who is best known for his pottery, has been credited with forming the first correct explanation of the general water cycle. His ideas were based on observations of nature. Palissy stated that rainfall was the only source for rivers and streams. He argued that streams could not come from seawater or

Figure 1.3 German Jesuit scholar Athanasius Kircher's "Mundus Subterraneous" (1665) depicts how people once believed water circulated between the sea and the mountains. Blue-tinted flows are from mountains to the sea, while black represents subterranean flows from the sea to the mountains.

from air that turned to water underground. Palissy believed that the Sun caused water to rise, which formed clouds, and eventually it fell again as rain. The rain fell on mountains, seeping through cracks in the ground. The water moved downward until it reached an area blocked by rock. From here, the water found an opening and flowed from the ground as a river or stream.

Unfortunately, Palissy wrote in French at a time when most scientists read in Latin. Consequently, Palissy's views were not widely known, and erroneous Greek and Roman theories continued.

FROM PHILOSOPHIES TO EXPERIMENTATION

The approach to science began to change in the middle of the seventeenth century. Earlier philosophers thought and wrote about their ideas. In the seventeenth century, experimentation gradually became an important part of testing scientific ideas.

Pierre Perrault

Pierre Perrault (1608–1680) was an important pioneer in water-cycle science because his ideas were based on experiments. He measured the amount of water flowing in a small portion of the upper Seine River in Burgundy, France. He then determined the volume of rainwater that would drain into this same portion of the river. Perrault found that only one-sixth of the amount of rain that fell was needed to supply the flow for the river for a year. Although it is notable that Perrault determined a relationship between river flow and rainfall, some of the conclusions in his book, *On the Origin of Springs,* were incorrect. For instance, he felt that rainwater could not seep too far into the ground. Additionally, he thought that rivers fed springs, rather than the other way around.

Edmé Mariotte

Edmé Mariotte (1620–1684) is best known for discovering the blind spot in the human eye. He also made an important contribution to the history of hydrology. He included a section entitled, "On the Origin of Springs," in his *Treatise on the Movement of the Waters and of the Other Fluid Bodies*. In this work, Mariotte explained that the water collected in the bottom of **wells**—holes dug or drilled in the ground to obtain water—came from rainfall. When the rain fell on the ground, it seeped into Earth through small channels. When rainfall on hills and mountains seeped into the ground, Mariotte said it often flowed into a rock or clay layer. Because the water could not pass through this layer, it continued its downward journey by flowing along the surface of the layer. When the water found a weak spot in the layer, it flowed out of the hill and formed springs.

Mariotte felt that rainfall was the obvious source of springs. He noted that springs decrease or dry up during dry periods and increase during wet periods. Mariotte rejected previous ideas, like those proponed by Perrault and Seneca, that rainfall could not seep into the ground. He based his rejection of these ideas on his observation of increased water flow into the cellars of the Royal Observatory in Paris after heavy rains.

Mariotte expanded on Perrault's earlier study of the Seine River. His analysis determined the rainfall over a much larger land area, thus providing for a larger drainage area into the river. Additionally, Mariotte used wax floats to more precisely calculate the river flow. He accomplished these calculations by measuring the time it took for a float to be carried a known distance down the river. Through this process, Mariotte mathematically confirmed that there was enough rainfall to supply the flow for rivers and springs.

Edmond Halley

British astronomer Edmond Halley (1656–1741) is best known for his calculation of the orbit of the comet now called "Halley's Comet." He also made an important contribution to the understanding of the water cycle by studying evaporation. In fact, Halley was the first scientist to estimate evaporation and to show its significance as part of the water cycle. He heated a pan of water for two hours until it reached the summertime air temperature. To determine how much water had evaporated, he compared the weight of the water in the pan to its weight before the heating process. Halley concluded that about 0.10 inches (0.25 centimeters) evaporated each day. From this value, he estimated the evaporation from the Mediterranean Sea. Halley continued this analysis by estimating the amount of water that flowed into the Mediterranean Sea from nine rivers. He showed that there was enough water evaporating from the Mediterranean Sea to supply the flow of water into the sea from rivers.

John Dalton

Even a century after Perrault, Mariotte, and Halley had completed their work, there was still no unanimous acceptance of the water-cycle concept. To tackle this problem, John Dalton (1766–1844) presented the first large-scale water balance for England and Wales in 1802. A water balance determines the flow of water into and out of an area. Dalton intended to show that the amount of rain and **dew** (water that has condensed onto objects near the ground) entering a region equaled the amount of river flow and evaporation leaving the region. Dalton estimated each of these four components separately using the rainfall from 30 separate rain gauges across England and Wales. His work produced one of the most complete sets of data that had been compiled at the time. Dalton's results showed that 36 inches (91.4 cm) of water entered the region and that 43 inches (109.2 cm) left the region. Therefore, his study resulted in an imbalance of 7 inches (17.8 cm). Most of this difference resulted from an overestimation of the evaporation and problems with the evaporation measurements.

Dalton stated in his summary that he could finally conclude that rain and dew are equal to the water carried off by evaporation and river flow. He stated that rain is the source of springs, not vast underground reservoirs or seawater that gets filtered as it rises to the ground surface. Therefore, at the beginning of the nineteenth century, Dalton effectively put to rest the ancient ideas of the source of rivers and springs under discussion for more than 2,000 years.

Modern Understanding of the Water Cycle

Water is a unique substance. It can be found in all three phases—solid, liquid, and gas—at the temperatures found on Earth. Its unique properties allow movement between the reservoirs of the water cycle, including the land surface, oceans, atmosphere, and underground.

Water is commonly known as H_2O, which means that a water molecule is made of two hydrogen atoms and one oxygen atom. An **atom** is the smallest part of a chemical element that has the characteristics of that element. Atoms are often called the basic building blocks of matter. In water, two hydrogen atoms are attached to the same side of an oxygen atom. This gives the hydrogen side of water molecules a positive charge and the oxygen side a negative charge. Because opposite charges attract, the hydrogen side of one water molecule attracts the oxygen side of another. Whether water exists as a solid, liquid, or gas depends on how tightly its molecules are bound together.

WATER'S PHASE CHANGE

Water molecules are in constant motion. This motion occurs within all three phases. Even molecules within a frozen cube of ice are moving. At higher temperatures, molecules move faster, and at lower temperatures they move slower. In each of the three phases, however, the molecules are arranged differently.

In ice, low temperatures mean that the water molecules have little energy available. With little energy, they cannot move fast. The molecules in ice vibrate in place, but they cannot move about freely. The bonds between water molecules remain strong, thus allowing the molecules to form an orderly pattern. As the temperature rises, the molecules vibrate faster. The bonds between some of the water molecules weaken, and the ice starts to melt.

Bonds are not firmly set in the liquid phase. Water molecules can slide past each other. This action allows water in the liquid phase to flow and take the shape of its container. As the temperature rises, more energy is available, and molecules move faster. The bonds between water molecules break, and the molecules escape from the water surface as a gas, called **water vapor**. In the gas phase, the molecules of water vapor move quickly in a disorganized manner.

When the temperature decreases, water molecules slow down, and the bonds form between molecules. Gases change to liquids, and liquids change to solids.

DEVELOPMENT OF GAS LAWS AND KINETIC THEORY OF GASES

Modern science recognizes heat as a measurement of the motion of molecules. The molecules of hot substances move faster than the molecules of cold substances. Yet at the beginning of the eighteenth century, scientists believed heat was a physical substance, such as fluid, contained within materials. The word they used for this substance is *caloric*.

By 1810, John Dalton had made one of the first advances in disproving the caloric theory of heat by developing the atomic theory of matter, which stated that elements are made of tiny particles called atoms. All atoms of the same element have the same chemical properties. Dalton further explained that atoms of different elements have different properties. No atoms of any element disappear or are changed into atoms of another element in chemical reactions.

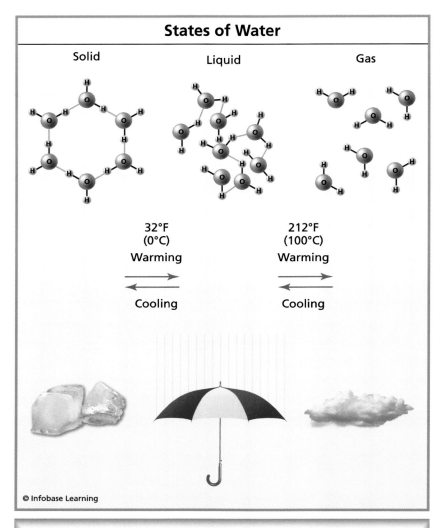

Figure 2.1 Water can exist in all three physical states: solid, liquid, and gas. In the solid state, water molecules are held together in a crystalline lattice. In the liquid state, water molecules move about relatively freely. In the gaseous state, water molecules move even more freely and tend to distribute themselves randomly.

Dalton also determined that specific ratios of elements combine to form compounds.

The development of the gas laws was another step in recognizing that heat is a physical rather than chemical property of a molecule.

The gas laws are a series of relationships between basic gas properties as follows:

- In 1660, Robert Boyle (1627–1691) established the relationship of pressure (P) to volume (V) in a gas. Boyle's Law can be written as $P_2V_2 = P_1V_1$.
- In 1787, Jacques Charles (1746–1823) determined the relationship between the temperature and volume of a gas. Joseph Gay-Lussac (1778–1850) expanded Charles' work in 1802 by determining the exact mathematic relationship. When temperature increases 33.8° Fahrenheit (1° Celsius), the volume of the gas increases by 1/273 of its value at 32°F (0°C). The relationship can be written as $V = V_0(1 + t/273)$, where V is the volume at temperature, t, in degrees Celsius, and V_0 is the volume at 32°F (0°C).
- In 1811, Amedeo Avogadro (1776–1856) found that equal volumes of all gases contain the same number of molecules at the same temperature and pressure.

The work of Boyle, Charles, Gay-Lussac, and Avogadro led to the Ideal Gas Law, which defines a relationship between temperature, volume, and pressure. This relationship can be written as PV = nRT, where P is pressure, V is volume, n is the number of moles of gas, R is a constant, and T is temperature. A mole is a unit that contains Avogadro's number of things (6.022×10^{23}). Avogadro's number is extremely large and not useful for counting everyday, ordinary objects. However, this large number becomes very useful when counting extremely small objects, such as atoms and molecules. For example, one mole of oxygen (O) atoms equals 6.022×10^{23} O atoms. One mole of water (H_2O) molecules equals 6.022×10^{23} H_2O molecules. Likewise, one mole of pennies equals 6.022×10^{23} pennies, which totals $6,022,000,000,000,000,000,000.00.

The development of the kinetic theory of gases provided more crucial evidence in support of the physical property of heat. In about 1866, James Clerk Maxwell (1831–1879) and Ludwig Boltzmann (1844–1906) proposed a relationship between the temperature and movement of particles in gas called the kinetic theory of gases. They demonstrated that the temperature of a gas indicates the average movement of gas molecules. Increased speed of the molecules causes more collisions between molecules. Therefore, the pressure increases as temperature increases.

The kinetic theory of gases was one of the major scientific discoveries of the nineteenth century. Its development was possible because of the development of the atomic theory of matter and the gas laws. These nineteenth century developments form the foundation of our modern understanding of water's phase changes.

PROCESSES OF THE WATER CYCLE

During water's journey through the water cycle—from oceans to the atmosphere to the surface of the land to the underground—water changes states between solid, liquid, and gas. Processes within the water cycle allow phase changes to take place. These processes are responsible for water's movement from one reservoir to another.

Evaporation and Transpiration

Evaporation occurs when water changes from a liquid to a gas. Evaporation moves water from the land, oceans, lakes, ponds, and rivers into the atmosphere. Most of the water in the atmosphere evaporates from oceans. In fact, the National Aeronautics and Space Administration estimates that oceans provide 86% of water vapor in the atmosphere. More water vapor is present at lower elevations than at higher elevations in the atmosphere because Earth is the source of the moisture.

Evaporation from plants is called **transpiration**. Water is taken from the soil through a plant's roots. It moves up the plant and is released into the air through pores on the plant's leaves. Scientists often view evaporation and transpiration together, referring to the sum as **evapotranspiration**.

For water to evaporate, the water molecules need enough energy to break the bonds of the liquid and form vapor. Heat that is absorbed from the environment provides this needed energy. This heat is called latent heat. The heat is latent, or "hidden," because adding heat does not change the temperature; instead, the heat can be thought of as being "stored" by the vapor. Evaporation is a **cooling process**. The hotter, faster-moving water molecules break their bonds and evaporate first. The remaining molecules have a lower average energy (temperature).

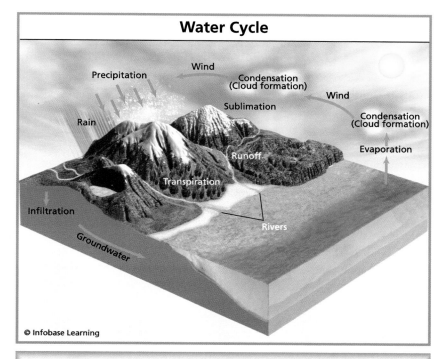

Water Cycle

Precipitation

Wind

Condensation
(Cloud formation)

Wind

Condensation
(Cloud formation)

Sublimation

Rain

Evaporation

Runoff

Transpiration

Infiltration

Rivers

Groundwater

© Infobase Learning

Figure 2.2   The major processes that drive the water cycle include precipitation, transpiration, evaporation, condensation, and infiltration.

Evaporation causes the cold feeling that a person experiences after getting out of a pool or shower. The water takes the energy, or heat, it needs to evaporate from the skin. This process leaves the skin cooler, maybe even cold enough to form goose bumps.

Condensation

Condensation is the change of state from water vapor (gas) to liquid. Clouds, fog, and dew are the most visible examples of condensation in nature. Condensation is likely to occur when the air cools and when vapor molecules slow down. The temperature at which water vapor begins to condense is the **dew point**.

For condensation to take place, the water vapor must have an object on which it can condense. On a cold day, condensation is seen on the inside surface of windows in a heated room. The cold glass cools the air, causing the water to condense on the glass. Even in the air, water condenses on dust and other small particles to form clouds.

When water condenses, it gives up heat. Therefore, condensation is called a **warming process**.

Precipitation

Any form of water, solid or liquid, that falls from the atmosphere to the ground is **precipitation**, including rain, snow, hail, sleet, or even

Development of Cloud Classification

Although many of the constellations, such as Orion, were named by ancient astronomers, cloud types had no names until the nineteenth century. Before then, it was thought that clouds could not be identified because of their changing nature. People described clouds by their color and shape as they saw them.

In 1803, a London pharmacist, Luke Howard (1772–1864), identified four basic cloud forms. He gave them Latin names to describe their appearance from the ground. This classification system was similar to the system for naming animals and plants. These names were *cumulus* (heaped), *stratus* (layered, sheetlike), *cirrus* (feathered, wispy), and *nimbus* (rain-bearing). Other cloud names were formed by combining the basic names.

This cloud classification system was not the first one that had been introduced. In 1802, Frenchman Jean-Baptiste Lamarck (1744–1829) proposed a system based on five types of clouds; however, he classified his cloud names in French at a time when Latin was the scholarly language used. Lamarck's system did not gain acceptance, even in France. Interestingly, four of the five cloud types in Lamarck's naming system appear in Howard's system but with different names.

Howard's classification system was expanded in 1887 by Ralph Abercromby (1842–1897) and Hugo Hildebrandsson

virga—rain that evaporates before it reaches the ground. Precipitation is the end result of a number of processes, including the evaporation of water from the land surface, the rising of warm air, the cooling and expansion of the air, and condensation into droplets in clouds. Water droplets join together and fall as rain (precipitation) when the droplets become too heavy to remain suspended.

Precipitation is the source of all water on Earth's surface; however, the amounts of precipitation vary across Earth. Lack of rain causes droughts in some areas, whereas other areas experience a **flood** from an overabundance of rain.

(1838–1925). This system is used today with minor modifications. Ten basic cloud types are recognized internationally. They are classified on the basis of form and the height at which they appear in the atmosphere.

The three cloud forms are cirrus, cumulus, or stratus. Nimbus is not considered a form in the classification system; instead, it is a condition of bearing rain and is included in cloud names such as nimbostratus and cumulonimbus.

The second part of cloud classification is height and includes three levels: high, middle, and low. (Table 2.1 outlines the types of clouds by height.) Clouds of vertical development have bases in the low elevations and heights that extend into the upper levels.

Table 2.1. Cloud Types by Height in the Atmosphere	
Cloud Types	
(1) High Clouds • Cirrus • Cirrostratus • Cirrocumulus	(3) Low Clouds • Stratus • Stratocumulus • Nimbostratus
(2) Middle Clouds • Altocumulus • Altostratus	(4) Clouds of Vertical Development • Cumulus • Cumulonimbus

After precipitation reaches the ground, it may be stored on the land surface in puddles, ponds, and lakes. It may run off to another place to be stored or flow into a stream. Some will soak into the ground to be stored. Plants will use part of the water that soaks in. Some of the falling precipitation will immediately return to the atmosphere through evaporation.

Infiltration

Infiltration is the movement of water from the land surface into the soil. Many people mistakenly believe that water collects in underground lakes or streams—which seems logical. In caves, water can

Drought: An Extreme of the Water Cycle

Drought is a long period of abnormally dry weather. It is basically a lack of rain or snow. The effects of drought build up over time instead of causing sudden destruction, like with hurricanes and earthquakes. Thus, droughts often are not considered to be as serious as other natural disasters, yet the devastation caused by drought can cost more than other natural disasters. The National Drought Mitigation Center estimates that damage from drought costs $6 to $8 billion per year in the United States. In comparison, floods cost $2.4 billion per year, and hurricanes cost $1.2 to $4.8 billion per year.

Many people consider drought to be a rare event. However, it is actually a normal, repeating part of a region's climate. Our technology used to measure drought only gives about 100 years of recorded data. In this time, there have been droughts in the 1930s (often called the **Dust Bowl**), the 1950s, and the period from 1987–1989. Using tree rings to reconstruct drought over 300 years shows that drought similar to the one in the 1950s occurred one or two times per century in the 1730s, 1820s, and 1860s. Longer-term be seen flowing freely in underground streams; however, the reality of this underground reservoir is much different. It is not a large, underground pool or pond; instead, it is water filling cracks in rocks and open spaces between soils and rocks underground.

These open spaces, called pores, are formed because grains of soil, rock, and sediment do not fit perfectly together. As water infiltrates, or soaks, into the ground, it first moves through an area where both air and water fill the pore spaces. This area is called the unsaturated zone. As water seeps deeper into the ground, it finally reaches an area where every pore is filled with water. This area is called the saturated zone. The water that reaches the saturated zone is called groundwater. The **water table** is the boundary between the saturated and unsaturated zones.

records show that more severe droughts occurred in North America in the last half of the sixteenth century than in the 1930s Dust Bowl. A review of 2,000 years of data shows that even the sixteenth century drought is relatively mild compared to other droughts in the 2,000-year time frame. Some experts even think drought caused the collapse of the Mayan civilization in A.D. 800–900.

No clear definition of drought exists. The definition used depends on the way drought is measured. A *meteorological drought* is based on the amount of dryness and length of the dry period. An *agricultural drought* measures the effects of dryness on agriculture, including reduced soil moisture, evapotranspiration, groundwater and reservoir levels, and any other factors that could affect agriculture. A *hydrological drought* measures the effects of dryness on surface water and underground water supplies. It is measured through river flows and the levels of lakes and underground water supplies. A *socioeconomic drought* occurs when there is a greater demand for goods than what can be supplied because of water shortages. This supply and demand can apply to anything from grain to fish to **hydroelectric power**—electricity produced by flowing or falling water.

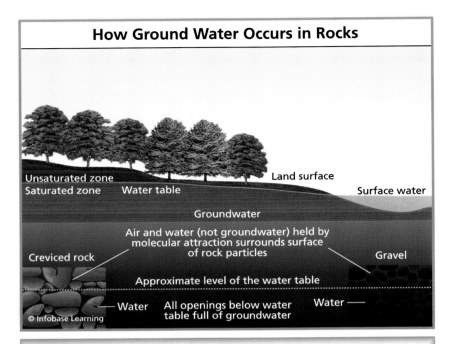

How Ground Water Occurs in Rocks

Unsaturated zone
Saturated zone   Water table
Land surface
Surface water

Groundwater

Air and water (not groundwater) held by
molecular attraction surrounds surface
of rock particles

Creviced rock

Gravel

Approximate level of the water table

© Infobase Learning

Water   All openings below water
table full of groundwater
Water

Figure 2.3   Groundwater easily seeps into the earth through dirt, crevices in rocks, and more. It settles down into the saturated zone.

Runoff

The part of precipitation that flows across the ground surface and winds up in streams is called **runoff**. The type of ground coverage and land use affects runoff. Although water infiltrates into land covered by vegetation, it runs off pavements, sidewalks, and rooftops. Runoff carries excess rainwater to streams and rivers, which eventually flow to the ocean. In overland and stream flow processes, water carves and shapes the landscape.

Sublimation and Deposition

Water can change from ice (solid) to water vapor (gas) without going through the liquid phase first. This process is called **sublimation**. It happens more frequently under conditions of low humidity and dry winds. It is also more common in high elevations with low air pressure. For example, the **Chinook wind** is a warm, dry wind that blows down the eastern slope of the Rocky Mountains. Air compresses and warms as it descends from the mountains. As it blows over heavy snow cover, the snow sublimates. Over a foot of snow a day has vanished due to the Chinook winds. For this reason, these winds are often called snow eaters. Sublimation absorbs heat, thus cooling the environment.

Deposition is the change from water vapor (gas) to ice (solid) without going through the liquid phase. It is the opposite of sublimation. Snow is formed in the clouds by deposition. In addition, the tiny ice crystals that make up **frost** are formed by deposition. Heat is released when deposition occurs.

PATHWAYS THROUGH THE WATER CYCLE

The movement of water through the water cycle can take several paths. The path that the water takes determines how long it stays in an area. The average time water stays in the atmosphere is 10 days. A drop of water that falls on a pasture may evaporate back to the atmosphere in a few hours or days, or the drop may hit the ground and flow into a puddle. From the puddle, it may infiltrate into the ground. The drop could also flow downhill (runoff) to a stream and finally into the ocean. The average time that water stays in rivers is 16–26 days. Some water has probably been frozen in ice fields in Greenland for thousands of years.

Water moves more slowly underground than it does over land and in the atmosphere. A drop of water seeping underground will most likely evaporate back to the atmosphere from the soil or transpire back through plants. In either case, the drop of water usually stays underground less than a year. The water drop could flow back to surface water bodies within a few days to months after infiltration. A drop of water that infiltrates all the way down in the **aquifer** may stay there for days or thousands of years.

Throughout the different pathways of the water cycle, the total amount of water on Earth remains the same. Table 2.2 shows an estimate of the global water supply as it moves through the water cycle.

Table 2.2 Estimated Global Water Supply			
Water Source	Water Volume (cubic miles)	Water Volume (cubic kilometers)	Total Percentage of Water (%)
Oceans, seas, and bays	321,000,000	1,338,000,000	96.5
Ice caps, glaciers, and permanent snow	5,773,000	24,064,000	1.74
Groundwater • Fresh • Saline	5,614,000 2,526,000 3,088,000	23,400,000 10,530,000 12,870,000	1.7 0.76 0.94
Soil moisture	3,959	16,500	0.001
Ground ice and permafrost	71,970	300,000	0.022
Lakes • Fresh • Saline	42,320 21,830 20,490	176,400 91,000 85,400	0.013 0.007 0.006
Atmosphere	3,095	12,900	0.001
Swamp water	2,752	11,470	0.0008
Rivers	509	2,120	0.0002
Biological water	269	1,120	0.0001
Total	332,600,000	1,386,000,000	100

THE WATER BUDGET

A **water budget** is a tool that scientists use to account for the different parts of the water cycle. The basic principle of a water budget is that the amount of water stored in an area is the difference between that flowing in and that leaving the area. A simplified water budget equation can be expressed as follows:

$\Delta S = P + Q_{in} - ET - R,$
where
ΔS = change in storage,
P = precipitation,
Q_{in} = water flowing into an area,
ET = evapotranspiration, and
R = runoff from the area.

Water in the Atmosphere

The sky would be a different place without water in the atmosphere. There would be no clouds—nothing to see but clear, blue skies. Without clouds, electrical charges would have no place to build, so there would be no bright flashes of lightning. Without lightning, there would be no thunder. The skies would be silent. Without water in the atmosphere, the Sun's rays would not bend to form a rainbow's bright spectrum of colors.

MEASURING ATMOSPHERIC MOISTURE

Relative humidity is one of the most common measurements of water in the atmosphere, yet it is also one of the most misunderstood. It can be confusing because it does not actually measure the amount of water vapor in the air. Relative humidity, which is written as a percentage, compares the amount of water vapor in the air to the amount required for **saturation**. Saturation is the maximum amount of water vapor the air can hold at a particular temperature and pressure. Thus, relative humidity measures how near the air is to saturation rather than the amount of moisture in the air.

The dew point temperature, which is shortened to *dew point*, is another common measurement of humidity. It is the temperature to which air must be cooled to reach saturation. As the name implies, cooling below the dew point causes water vapor to condense, thus forming dew and fog. Unlike the relative humidity measurement, the dew point measures the actual amount of water vapor in the air. Therefore, it is very useful in measuring humidity in the air. The water vapor content is high when the dew point is high. Low dew points mean low water vapor content. Adding water vapor to the air raises the dew point, and removing water vapor lowers it.

Comparing the air temperature with the dew point temperature indicates whether the relative humidity is high or low. A big difference between air temperature and dew point temperature means that relative humidity is low. If air temperature and dew point temperature are close, the relative humidity is high. At 100% relative humidity, the air and dew point temperatures are the same.

FORMATION OF DEW AND FOG

The feel of wet grass early in the morning is a reminder of how water changes phases. After the Sun goes down, the ground loses heat. On cloudy nights, clouds absorb this heat and send it back downward allowing temperatures to stay warm. On clear nights, the heat is lost to space, and the ground becomes cooler. Air that touches the ground cools, often to its dew point. As grass and leaves cool below this temperature, water vapor condenses on them. These water droplets are called dew. Many plants in dry areas survive because of dew. If the temperature drops below freezing, dew will freeze into tiny beads of ice called frozen dew.

Frost is ice crystals that form on surfaces instead of dew when the dew point is below freezing. Frost is also called white frost or hoar frost. It looks like branches, whereas frozen dew is shaped like beads. Frost is formed by deposition. Water vapor changes directly into ice without passing through the liquid phase. A pattern of frost ice crystals often decorates windows in the winter.

FORMATION OF FOG

Fog is a cloud resting at or very near the ground. Fog hinders visibility. It makes it difficult for airplanes to take off or land, and it often causes multiple car collisions on highways. There is no physical difference between fog and a cloud. The main difference is how and where each forms. Although all fog looks the same, it is formed in two different ways. Most fog forms when humid air cools to its dew point, condensing water vapor into tiny drops. Some fog forms when enough water is added to the air by evaporation to reach saturation.

Fogs Formed by Cooling

Advection is the horizontal movement of air. When wind pushes warm, humid air over cold ground, the air loses its heat to the ground below. If the air cools to its dew point, condensation will occur in the form of advection fog.

Radiation fog forms much in the same way that dew forms. On clear nights, the ground cools, thus chilling the air near it. When the relative humidity is high, a small amount of cooling lowers the temperature to the dew point; this process results in fog. Radiation fog is thickest in valleys. As the air cools it becomes dense and heavy and drains downhill. These fogs often "burn off" within 1 to 3 hours after sunrise. Although the fog is often said to "lift," it does not really rise; instead, the rising Sun warms the ground, evaporating the fog from the bottom up.

Upslope fog occurs when wind blows humid air up a hill or mountain. As the air moves upward, it expands and cools. When the dew point is reached, fog forms.

Evaporation Fogs

Steam fog forms when cold air blows over warm water. Water rapidly evaporates from the surface, saturating the cold air above. Vapor condenses into droplets and looks like steam rising from the water surface.

Evaporation, or frontal, fog occurs when warm rain falls into cooler, drier air near the ground. Evaporation of the raindrops increases the humidity of the cool air layer, forming fog.

FORMATION OF CLOUDS

A concern in the eighteenth century was why clouds floated and did not fall. People knew that clouds were made of water and that water

Figure 3.1   Fog is a collection of water droplets or ice crystals suspended in air near Earth's surface. It forms when water vapor condenses in the air.

was heavier than air. One suggestion was that the clouds formed from bubbles of water, similar to soap bubbles. Because bubbles are filled with air, they felt that this would explain why clouds floated. In the nineteenth century, Augustus Waller observed cloud droplets on spider webs. He confirmed that clouds were made of drops of water—not bubbles.

The condensation process that produces clouds in the air is not quite as simple as that for dew and frost. Water vapor needs a surface on which it can condense. For dew and frost, blades of grass or windows may serve this purpose. To form cloud droplets, the air must contain particles on which the water vapor can condense. These particles are called condensation nuclei. They include dust particles, smoke, pollen, sea salt, or anything else that may be in the air. Clouds are made of billions of droplets that are so tiny that they stay in the air. One raindrop contains about a million cloud droplets.

Warm air is less dense (lighter) than cold air and tends to rise. The pressure in the atmosphere decreases with height. As air rises, it experiences this decrease in pressure. Following the gas laws, the air expands and cools. (Likewise, when air is compressed, it warms.) When air cools to its dew point temperature, clouds develop.

Air tends to resist rising on its own. Air near the surface stays there unless it is forced to rise. **Topography** (the shape and features of the Earth's surface) is one of the reasons that air rises. Because horizontally moving air cannot pass through barriers, such as mountains, it is forced to rise over them. This is called orographic lifting. As the air climbs the mountain slope, it expands as the pressure decreases. If the air is humid, it will condense as it cools, forming clouds.

Fortunately for the flat areas of central North America, mountains are not the only cause of rising air. When warm and cold air masses collide, the colder, dense air acts as a barrier. The warmer, less dense air rises over the cold air, a process called frontal wedging. As a result the rising warm air cools and clouds form.

When air near the surface flows together, or converges, from different directions, it must have some place to go. The air cannot pile up where it meets. The ground blocks it from moving downward. Naturally, it must go upward. As it rises and cools, clouds form.

Some areas of Earth's surface heat more quickly than others. A parking lot, for instance, usually warms faster than a wooded area. The air above these warm spots heats and rises. These warm updrafts of air are called **thermals**. Birds, such as eagles and hawks, often ride these updrafts to great heights, using little energy in the process. Expansion and cooling of the rising air eventually forms clouds.

CLOUD IDENTIFICATION

The World Meteorological Organization recognizes ten basic types of clouds. They are classified by both their form and the height at

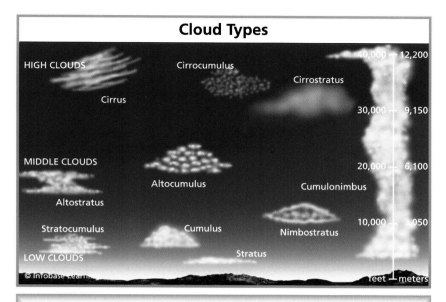

Cloud Types

HIGH CLOUDS

Cirrocumulus

Cirrostratus

Cirrus

40,000 — 12,200

30,000 — 9,150

MIDDLE CLOUDS

Altocumulus

Cumulonimbus

20,000 — 6,100

Altostratus

Stratocumulus

Cumulus

Nimbostratus

10,000 — 3,050

LOW CLOUDS

Stratus

© Infobase Learning

feet — meters

Figure 3.2 All cloud types fit into one of three altitude classes: low, medium, or high.

which they appear in the atmosphere. The three basic cloud forms are *cirrus*, which means "curl of hair," *cumulus*, which means "heap," and *stratus*, which means "layer." Height, the second part of cloud classification, is divided into four groups: high, middle, low, and clouds of vertical development.

High clouds typically have bases above 20,000 feet (6,096 meters). The term *cirrus*, or prefix *cirro*, indicates high clouds. The three types of high clouds are cirrus, cirrostratus, and cirrocumulus. At these high elevations, air is generally cold and dry. Therefore, high clouds are made mostly of ice crystals and are very thin.

Middle clouds appear between 6,500 and 20,000 feet (1,981 and 6,096 m). The Latin prefix, *alto*, identifies middle height clouds. The two types of middle clouds are altocumulus and altostratus. Middle clouds are made mostly of water droplets. They may contain some ice crystals when the temperature is cold enough.

Low clouds form below 6,500 feet (1,981 m). Their names do not include prefixes. The three types of low clouds are stratus, stratocumulus, and nimbostratus. Low clouds are usually made of water droplets and may contain ice or snow in cold weather.

Clouds of vertical development have bases in the low elevations. However, their height reaches into the middle or high ranges. The two types of clouds of vertical development are cumulus and cumulonimbus. Table 3.1 lists cloud groups, types, and characteristics.

Each cloud fits into only one of the ten basic cloud types. A descriptive word can be added to the name of clouds to better describe differences in the shape or form of each of the ten cloud types. Table 3.2 provides a few examples of descriptive words that are used to identify clouds.

Interestingly, there is an increase in reported unidentified flying objects and flying saucer sightings when lenticular clouds are present. They usually form when moist air crosses a mountain region. The shape of lenticular clouds can resemble an almond or a stack of pancakes.

CONTRAILS: MAN-MADE CLOUDS

Contrails are the white line-shaped clouds produced by jet aircraft. The name comes from *con*densation *trail*. Contrails are mainly made of ice crystals because they form at high elevations where the temperatures are cold. Contrails form in the same manner as other clouds form. Water vapor, contained in the jet engine exhaust, reaches saturation. The particles in the exhaust often supply the nuclei needed for condensation to occur. Contrails evaporate quickly when the surrounding air is dry. If the relative humidity is high—the air is near saturation—the contrails may last for several hours.

PRECIPITATION

The formation of clouds alone is not enough to cause rain. All clouds are made of water, but not all clouds produce rain. Cloud droplets are tiny and fall very slowly. In unsaturated air, the cloud droplets would evaporate again before falling very far from the base of the cloud. It takes about a million cloud droplets to form one raindrop that is heavy enough to fall. Condensation alone is too slow to produce

(continues on page 42)

Table 3.1 Basic Cloud Types

Cloud Group	Cloud Type	Characteristic
Low (bases greater than 6,500 ft or 1,981 m)	Stratus	Gray cloud layer resembling fog but not touching the ground; may produce drizzle
	Stratocumulus	Soft gray clouds appearing as rounded masses or rolls
	Nimbostratus	Layer of dark gray clouds; one of the primary rain-producing clouds
Middle (bases from 6,500–20,000 ft or 1,981–6,096 m)	Altostratus	Formless, gray cloud sheet covering all or most of the sky; the Sun is usually at least slightly visible through these clouds as a bright spot
	Altocumulus	White to gray clouds made of regularly arranged elements, often made of rounded masses resembling fleece
High (bases greater than 20,000 ft or 6,096 m)	Cirrus	White, wispy clouds of ice crystals with a hairlike appearance and often curled; called mares' tails when blown by the wind into the shape of streamers
	Cirrostratus	Thin, white ice-crystal clouds that form a veil or sheet; often produces a halo around the Sun or Moon
	Cirrocumulus	Ice-crystal clouds that may be formed by lumpy masses, rounded puffs, or rippled rows
Clouds of vertical development	Cumulus	Billowy clouds with flat bases and tops that resemble cauliflower or popcorn; often called fair weather clouds
	Cumulonimbus	Dark, billowy clouds in the form of towers, usually with an anvil-shaped top; produces heavy precipitation, lightning, thunder, and occasional hail

Table 3.2 Descriptive Terms for Identifying Clouds	
TERM	DESCRIPTION
Arcus	Cloud shaped like an arc
Calvus	Bald, cumulonimbus clouds that are losing their sprouting cauliflower structure
Castellanus	Clouds with towering structures that resemble small castles
Capillatus	Cumulonimbus clouds with hairy, fibrous, or striated tops
Congestus	Cumulus clouds with sprouting, towering structures that resemble cauliflower
Fractus	Clouds with a fractured, torn, or ragged appearance
Humilis	Humble, flat cumulus clouds
Incus	An anvil-shaped cloud in the upper part of a cumulonimbus
Lenticularis	Lens- or almond-shaped clouds
Mammatus	Clouds that hang from the underside of clouds like pouches
Pileus	Clouds shaped like a hood or cap above, or attached to, the upper part of a cumulus cloud
Translucidus	Clouds that cover a large part of the sky but are transparent enough for the Sun or Moon to show through
Tuba	Tube- or trumpet-shaped clouds often associated with tornadoes or water spouts
Uncinus	Hook-shaped, streaky cirrus clouds that look like a comma laying on its side
Undulatus	Clouds with wavelike features

Figure 3.3   A lenticular wind cloud resembling a flying saucer floats over Peavine Mountain near Reno, Nevada. These kinds of lens-shaped clouds form at high altitudes, often perpendicular to the direction of wind.

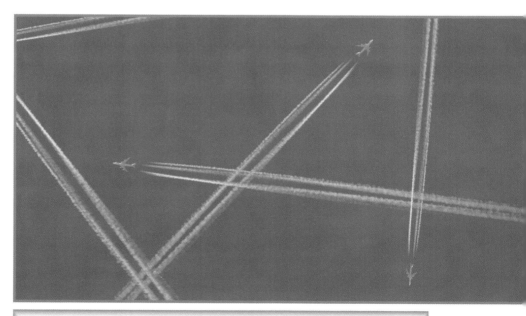

Figure 3.4   Contrails, short for "condensation trails," are trails of condensed water made by the exhaust of aircraft engines.

(continued from page 38)

raindrops. Some other processes must be working to produce rain. Scientists are still working to understand the processes that form rain. They believe that rain is produced differently in warm and cold clouds.

In warm clouds, rain is formed by the collision-coalescence process in which larger droplets collide with, and stick to, smaller droplets. The larger droplets continue to grow until they are heavy enough to fall from the cloud.

In cold clouds, rain is formed by the ice-crystal, or Bergeron, process. In these clouds, **supercooled water** droplets remain as a liquid even though temperatures are below freezing. Ice crystals are

Cloud Seeding

"The Man Who Can Make It Rain" is what a 1947 article in the *Saturday Evening Post* called Vincent Schaefer (1906–1993). He worked at the General Electric Laboratory in Schenectady, NY, with Chemistry Nobel Prize winner, Dr. Irving Langmuir (1881–1957). While researching aircraft icing during World War II, Langmuir and Schaefer noticed that supercooled clouds (below 32° Fahrenheit [0° Celsius]) contained almost no ice crystals. Wondering if the cause was a lack of nuclei, Schaefer set up a simple laboratory experiment. He lined a freezer with black velvet and breathed into the cold air inside. For weeks, he added powdered materials, including sulfur, sand, carbon, and talcum powder, to the cloud droplets created in the freezer by his breath in an attempt to form snow. On a hot day in July 1946, the freezer would not cool enough to create a cloud from his breath. Schaefer added dry ice (frozen carbon dioxide) to lower the temperature inside the freezer. To his surprise, ice crystals immediately formed in the cloud of breath in the freezer.

On November 13, 1946, Schaefer went up in an airplane and sprinkled dry ice onto a layer of clouds above in the clouds with the supercooled water droplets, although neither is large enough or heavy enough to fall. Water evaporates from the supercooled water drop and sticks to the ice crystals. This process allows the ice crystals to grow larger and heavy enough to fall. As a result, the water droplets become smaller.

Most people consider any falling water to be rain. From a meteorologist's standpoint, falling water is only rain if the diameter of the drops is over 0.02 inches (0.5 millimeters). Rain usually falls from nimbostratus or cumulonimbus clouds. If the drops are fine and fairly uniform with a diameter of less than 0.02 inches (0.51 mm), then it is drizzle. Stratus clouds usually produce drizzle. Sometimes streaks of falling precipitation seem to hang in the air, never reaching

New York. Shortly afterwards, snowflakes fell from the cloud. This experiment was the first breakthrough in modern weather modification.

Another breakthrough was made by Schaefer's colleague, Bernard Vonnegut (1914–1997). He discovered that silver iodide could "seed" supercooled clouds. Silver iodide has a crystal structure similar to that of ice crystals, and it is the main material used for seeding clouds today.

Cloud seeding is successfully used to improve visibility at a few airports in the northwest. Dry ice or silver iodide is applied to fog that is colder than 32°F (0°C). The water droplets in the fog change to ice crystals and fall out, clearing the visibility.

In August 2008, the Olympic opening ceremonies were held in China in a normally wet season. The Chinese government seeded the clouds to prevent rain from falling during the ceremonies by launching 1,104 cloud-seeding missiles into the Beijing sky from 21 launch sites. The purpose of this procedure was to allow clouds to rain out before the ceremonies began. Because it did not rain at Olympic National Stadium, Chinese meteorologists claimed that the weather modification effort was successful.

Figure 3.5 Images from *Studies among the Snow Crystals* (1902) by Wilson Bentley show the variation among snowflake shapes. Bentley, called "The Snowflake Man," was a Vermont farmer whose hobby was photographing snowflakes. He used microphotography to photograph more than 5000 snowflakes—none of which looked the same.

the ground. The precipitation evaporates while it is still in the air. This type of rain, as noted earlier, is called virga.

Snow is the precipitation of ice crystals that are often joined together into snowflakes. The crystal structure of snow allows it to

Figure 3.6 This photo shows a record-setting hailstone that was found by a ranch hand in Vivian, South Dakota, on July 23, 2010. The hailstone measured 8 inches (20.3 cm) in diameter and weighed 1 pound, 15 ounces (0.5 kg).

take several different shapes. Snow forms by deposition of water vapor directly into ice crystals. Much of the precipitation that reaches the ground actually begins its journey as snow. Conditions beneath the cloud can change snow into another form of precipitation before it reaches the ground.

A snowflake will melt if it falls through a warm layer of air. It will turn back into ice if it then falls through a layer of air below freezing. However, it will not refreeze into a snowflake again. A tiny, transparent ice pellet will form sleet. These ice pellets usually bounce when they hit the ground and make a tapping sound on windows.

The cold layer of air lying beneath a warm layer may not be thick enough to allow the drops to refreeze. Instead, the drops fall as supercooled water called **freezing rain**. When freezing rain hits the ground or another cold object, it forms a thin layer of ice. This

(continues on page 48)

The National Aeronautics and Space Administration's Aqua Mission

At 2:55 A.M. Pacific daylight time on May 4, 2002, the National Aeronautics and Space Administration's (NASA) Aqua satellite blasted off from California aboard a rocket. About an hour later, the satellite separated from the rocket and began orbiting Earth. *Aqua* is Latin for "water." The satellite was given this name because it collects information about all aspects of the water cycle, including evaporation from the oceans, water vapor in the atmosphere, cloud formation, precipitation, soil moisture, sea ice, land ice, and snow cover. The satellite also measures air, land, and water temperatures.

One of the scientific goals of the Aqua mission is to better understand water in Earth's climate system and the global water cycle. The Aqua satellite carries six instruments used to make its measurements and gather data. Five teams of scientists study these data and use them in weather forecasting, climate prediction, and even in agricultural planning.

The Aqua mission has improved scientists' ability to monitor greenhouse gases in the atmosphere. In the past, carbon dioxide, for instance, was measured from a single point at a monitoring station. Now, the Aqua systems can make maps of carbon dioxide levels across Earth, rather than at one place only. These measurements have shown carbon dioxide reaching higher levels each year since 2002.

Another greenhouse gas that the Aqua satellite measures is ozone, which helps block ultraviolet radiation from reaching Earth's surface. Scientists are using the data from this mission to track a hole in the ozone that developed years ago.

Monitoring forest fires is a practical application of the Aqua data. Because scientists receive the Aqua data close to real time, they use the information to determine the best location to send firefighters to handle fires. In addition, the

Figure 3.7   NASA's Aqua Satellite is tested by researchers before its 2002 boost into space.

Aqua satellite captures dust storms, hurricanes, typhoons, Arctic snowstorms, and volcano eruptions.

When the Aqua satellite launched in 2002, NASA expected it to last for 6 years. That time has passed, and the satellite is still collecting data. Based on the rate that fuel is used, NASA predicts that the Aqua satellite could last until the year 2017. This would give scientists 15 years of data collection on Earth's water cycle.

(continued from page 45)
coating makes roads extremely dangerous. The weight of this ice can break tree limbs and down power lines.

Hail is precipitation of irregular pellets or balls of ice more than 0.2 inches. (5 mm) in diameter. Ice rings build, which increases the size of a hailstone, as they move up and down in a severe thunderstorm. On July 23, 2010, the largest hailstone in diameter and weight in U.S. history was found in Vivian, South Dakota. The hailstone measured 8.0 inches (20.3 cm) in diameter and weighed 1.9375 pounds (878.8 grams). The hailstone had a circumference of 18.62 inches (47.3 cm).

Once precipitation falls to Earth as rain, snow, sleet, or hail, it is ready to begin its journey through the water cycle again.

Water in the Ground

Lightning flashes, thunder roars, and rain pounds the ground. Some of the rainwater evaporates. Part of it runs off to other areas. The rest soaks into the ground. Some of the water that soaks into the ground evaporates from the soil back into the air, and some is used by plants. The water that continues to seep deeper forms the underground reservoir of the water cycle. It's called groundwater.

People have depended on groundwater since ancient times. The qanats—hand-dug tunnels sloping downward slightly—of ancient Persia (present-day Iran) date back as far as 800 B.C. Each tunnel was only large enough to fit the person digging it. The top of the tunnel was usually dug into the water table in the foothills of mountains. The end of the qanat tunnel opened into an irrigation canal.

Water flowed by gravity from the water table to the bottom of the tunnel where it provided water for a village. Vertical shafts, or holes, were dug every 65 to 100 feet (20 to 30 meters) along the length of the tunnels. These shafts were used to remove the dirt that was dug out. They also provided air and light for the person digging the tunnel and gave access to the tunnel for later repairs. Qanats are still in use today in some parts of southwestern Asia and North Africa.

GROUNDWATER ON THE MOVE

Water is constantly moving through the water cycle. Groundwater is no exception. However, groundwater usually moves much more

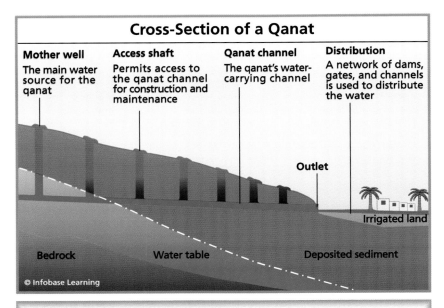

Cross-Section of a Qanat

Mother well	**Access shaft**	**Qanat channel**	**Distribution**
The main water source for the qanat	Permits access to the qanat channel for construction and maintenance	The qanat's water-carrying channel	A network of dams, gates, and channels is used to distribute the water

Outlet

Irrigated land

Bedrock   Water table   Deposited sediment

© Infobase Learning

Figure 4.1 A qanat is a gently sloping underground tunnel used for irrigation purposes.

slowly than water in the atmosphere or over land. Groundwater moves because gravity pulls it downward. Water flows from areas with high water tables to areas with lower water tables. It soaks into the ground and flows through the pores (spaces) between soils and rocks. The **porosity** of a soil or rock is the percentage of the open spaces inside the soil or rock. The porosity tells how much water the soil or rock can hold. Loosely packed soils have bigger spaces between their grains. Therefore, they have a higher porosity and can hold more water. Mud can have a porosity of 90% or more. Thus, it holds a lot of water in its pores, which explains why mud is wet. On the other hand, some rocks have almost no porosity and can hold little water.

Porosity defines how much water a soil or rock can hold if all the pores are filled with water. It does not explain how fast the water can flow through those pores. Water makes its way underground by winding between grains of soil and weaving through cracks. Smaller pore spaces make the path more difficult and generally slow the water flow. **Permeability** is the ability of a material to allow water to pass through it. Soils and rocks with higher permeability allow water to flow through them faster. Usually, as the porosity increases (pore spaces become greater), the permeability also increases. This is true if the pores are connected to each other. Water cannot flow from a pore that is completely surrounded by solid rock. If there is no connection between the pores, even a high porosity could not allow water movement.

Aquitards are layers of soil or rock that are not permeable or that hinder water movement. Clay is an example. In contrast, aquifers are underground areas in soil and rocks that can store and transmit large amounts of water to supply wells and springs. Aquifers are porous and permeable. When water is pumped out of an aquifer, more water flows in to replace it.

Much of the drinking water in the United States comes from groundwater aquifers. Both porosity and permeability are important in finding a usable groundwater supply. The best groundwater supplies are usually found in aquifers with a high porosity so that the soil and rock can store large amounts of water. Aquifers that supply groundwater also need to have a high permeability so that the water can move easily through the soil or rock when it is pumped to the surface for use as drinking water.

WATER SPRINGS FORTH

The sight of water "springing" from the ground with no obvious source has fascinated people for ages. A place where groundwater naturally flows out of the ground is a spring. It is where the water table meets the ground surface. As far back as written records exist, people wondered about the source of springs. In ancient times, springs were thought to come from oceans flowing underground. Others believed air entered the ground and condensed into water. With our current knowledge of groundwater science, these notions seem far-fetched today; however, people long ago did not understand the idea of rainwater recharging, or refilling, underground aquifers. Therefore, they could not grasp the concept that springs flow from groundwater reservoirs.

Groundwater can also rise to the surface in wells drilled into the aquifer. In most wells, groundwater does not rise on its own. It must

(continues on page 54)

Darcy's Law of Groundwater Flow

Our current understanding of groundwater movement began with French engineer Henry Darcy (1803–1858). Darcy's hometown of Dijon, France, had some of the filthiest water in Europe. Darcy was an engineer with Le Corps des Ponts et Chausseé, a French government agency in charge of bridges and highways.

Without being asked to do so, Darcy designed a water supply system for the city of Dijon. The city approved the design in 1835 without any changes. The water system went into operation in 1840. Rosoir Spring, located 7 miles (11 kilometers) upstream of Dijon, supplied water to the city through an aqueduct.

The water system included two reservoirs and a large fountain. Approximately 150 small fountains were located along the streets at about every 330 feet (101 m), giving the citizens access to freshwater. Dijon's water system was operating 25 years before the capital city of Paris had a water system. Darcy was offered a consultant's fee that would equal $1.5 million today. He refused the fee and instead accepted free water for life and a gold medal.

In 1856, Darcy published *Les Fontaines Publiques de la Ville de Dijon* (translated as "The Public Fountains of the City of Dijon") as an engineer's handbook for building water supply systems. Test results for laboratory experiments that he performed on a column of sand were tucked away in Appendix D of that handbook. The tests determined what factors influenced the rate that water flowed through sand, as follows:

- The steeper the slope of the water table, the faster water moves. The water table slope is called the hydraulic gradient.
- Groundwater flows more quickly through soils that have higher permeabilities than it does through those that have lower permeabilities. This factor is called hydraulic conductivity. It is a constant that is a property of the soil.
- **Darcy's Law**, the basic equation of groundwater flow, resulted from these experiments. The equation

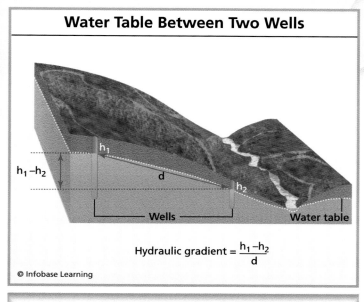

Water Table Between Two Wells

$$\text{Hydraulic gradient} = \frac{h_1 - h_2}{d}$$

© Infobase Learning

Figure 4.2 The hydraulic gradient is determined by measuring the difference in elevation between two points on the water table ($h_1 - h_2$) divided by the distance between them (d).

can be written in several different forms, but the following equation is one of the simplest forms:

$$Q = KA(H_1 - H_2)/D,$$

where

Q = discharge rate (volume that flows through an aquifer in a specified time),

A = cross-sectional area through which the water flows,

K = hydraulic conductivity (permeability of the aquifer),

D = flow distance,

$H_1 - H_2$ = difference in height (drop in water table), and

$(H_1 - H_2)/D$ = the calculated hydraulic gradient.

Darcy was the first person to determine a mathematical law for the flow of groundwater.

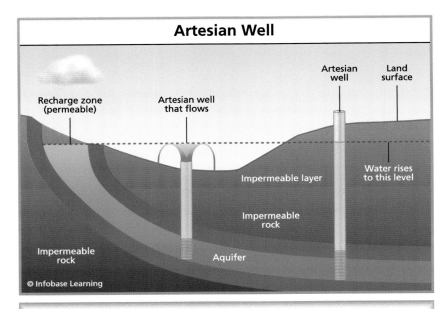

Artesian Well

Artesian well | Land surface

Recharge zone (permeable)

Artesian well that flows

Water rises to this level

Impermeable layer

Impermeable rock

Impermeable rock

Aquifer

© Infobase Learning

Figure 4.3 An artesian well is a well from which water flows under natural pressure without pumping.

(continued from page 51)

be pumped to the surface. Yet in artesian wells, water rises above the level of the aquifer. Artesian wells tap confined aquifers that have low permeability layers above and below them. The water in these aquifers is under enough pressure to cause it to rise. If the water rises above the ground surface, the well is called a flowing artesian well.

Artesian wells are named for the Artois region of France where these wells are common. Many bottled water companies advertise that their water comes from artesian wells. Yet the water in those bottles is basically no different from any other groundwater. The only true difference is that the water from artesian wells rises on its own and does not need to be pumped.

Groundwater can gush forth with spectacular eruptions from **geysers**. These are rare hot springs that periodically cause fountains of steam and hot water to erupt from a vent in the ground. Old Faithful in Yellowstone National Park is a famous example. Geysers erupt when groundwater seeps into underground chambers located in hot rock. The groundwater heats and expands. Some of the hot

Figure 4.4 Old Faithful Geyser spews boiling water and steam in Wyoming's Yellowstone National Park.

water and steam rises and erupts from the ground surface. After the eruption, cool groundwater seeps into the chamber again, and the process starts over.

THE POWER OF GROUNDWATER

As rainwater falls, it dissolves carbon dioxide from the atmosphere. When it seeps into the ground, it dissolves more carbon dioxide from decaying plants. As a result, carbonic acid is formed in the groundwater. This acid is the same acid that gives fizz to soft drinks, but the acid in groundwater is very weak. The acidic water seeps through cracks and pores in rock, dissolving minerals as it moves down to the water table. Over many thousands of years, openings are created. The water dissolves more limestone along cracks, enlarging the openings and forming networks of caves and caverns. These networks form below the water table where caves are filled with water, thus allowing walls, floors, and ceilings to dissolve.

When the water table falls, decoration of the caves begins. The caves, which had been filled with groundwater, become filled with air as water retreats. Water seeping through the soils above the cave oozes down through cracks in the ceiling. As the water drips, it leaves a small amount of the dissolved calcium carbonate on the ceiling of the cave. The deposits grow downward forming long iciclelike spikes of limestone hanging from the ceiling, called stalactites.

As the dripping water falls to the cave floor, it deposits calcium carbonate, forming mounds. Upward-pointing cones, called stalagmites, grow from the ground. When stalactites and stalagmites grow together, they form columns. Carlsbad Caverns in New Mexico is a popular tourist destination because of its beautiful cave formations. Another popular cave attraction is Mammoth Cave in Kentucky. With about 350 miles (563 km) of passages, Mammoth Cave is the world's longest-known cave.

Over many years, the carbonic acid in water can eat away holes in the ground surface. Sometimes the holes appear suddenly when the ground collapses through the roof of an underground cave. These depressions in the ground surface are called **sinkholes**. They are usually rounded or shaped like a cone. A sinkhole may be a few feet wide or hundreds of feet wide. If a sinkhole is large enough, it can swallow houses, roads, and even moving cars. Where one sinkhole is located, there are likely others because they form in limestone areas. Sinkholes can be caused by drought or by the overpumping of groundwater. When the water table drops, the water no longer supports the roof of the cave, and the land surface collapses into the cave.

A stream sometimes seems to disappear into the ground. In reality, the stream flows into a sinkhole, and from there, it continues its flow underground. Just as suddenly as it disappeared, the stream can reappear on the surface, sometimes miles away. These are called disappearing streams.

Karst topography is the unique landscape formed when water dissolves underground rocks, creating sinkholes, caves, underground drainage channels, and springs. "Karst" is a German word

Figure 4.5 An interior view of Carlsbad Caverns in Carlsbad Caverns National Park, New Mexico, shows stalactites and stalagmites.

that means "bare, stony ground." This type of topography is named for the Kras Plateau in Slovenia, along the eastern coast of the Adriatic Sea, which has caves and sinkholes throughout. Karst landforms often have groundwater pollution problems. Because of the large openings, surface water or stormwater flows underground quickly in karst areas. Therefore, the water does not get the chance to be naturally filtered by the soils.

Winter Park Sinkhole

At 8:00 P.M. on May 8, 1981, a resident of Winter Park, Florida, heard a swishing noise. She noticed that a large sycamore tree in her backyard had disappeared. When she went out to investigate, she found that a deep sinkhole had opened up around her home on West Comstock Avenue. It continued to grow. In two days, the sinkhole had swallowed her house, several sports cars, half of the city's Olympic-sized swimming pool, and a portion of Denning Drive. It grew to 348 feet (106 m) wide at the surface and 98 feet (30 m) deep. The sinkhole disrupted utilities, such as sanitary sewer and water lines, and upset traffic flow.

What had happened? The sinkhole seemed to develop suddenly. In reality, groundwater had been dissolving the underground limestone for a long time, and the dissolving process accelerated during the previous 50-year period. Large open spaces, or caves, had formed underground. The ground above the cave had been slowly crumbling into the cave for many years. In 1981, Winter Park experienced a drought, and the groundwater level was about 20 feet (6 m) lower than it had been 50 years earlier. The decline in water level over the previous 50 years was believed to be the cause of the rapid collapse of the ground into the cave.

The sinkhole was expected to continue growing unless something was done. Although it was dry when it first opened, the hole collected groundwater that rose to the level of the aquifer. The sinkhole was too large to be

PROBLEMS ASSOCIATED WITH USING GROUNDWATER

Groundwater Contamination

Many people now view fresh, pure groundwater as a limited resource. Groundwater can become unfit for use when harmful substances are

Figure 4.6 This aerial view shows a large sinkhole in Winter Park, Florida, on May 11, 1981. It continued to grow even as workers tried unsuccessfully to retrieve sunken sports cars from the depression. When it was finally stabilized and sealed, city planners decided to turn it into an urban lake.

completely filled in. City workers decreased the water level by 63 feet (19 m) by pumping water out of the sinkhole. The remainder of the swimming pool and its bathhouse were pushed into the hole. The center of the hole was filled with debris, and the side slopes were graded. Water levels were allowed to rise again. The sinkhole is now known as Lake Rose.

introduced into it. Most waters have some substances in them that are considered harmful. These substances are not a problem until they occur in high enough amounts to threaten human health or the environment. Some of the common sources of groundwater pollution include fuel and chemicals from leaking storage tanks, sewage from septic tanks and broken sewer pipes, barnyard wastes, wastes from leaking landfill liners, and agricultural fertilizers and pesticides.

Lowered Water Tables

If groundwater refills a well quicker than water is withdrawn from it, the water table will remain the same. If water is removed faster than groundwater can refill the well, the water table will drop around the area of the well. This effect is called drawdown. Drawdown is greatest at the well and lessens farther from the well. The water table takes the shape of a downward-pointing cone, called a cone of depression. If the water table drops too low, shallow wells can go dry. Low water tables can also cause springs and rivers to dry up.

Saltwater Intrusion

Freshwater exists under the land along coasts. Under the sea, the groundwater is salty. Freshwater is less dense than saltwater. In areas where the freshwater and salty groundwater meet, freshwater floats in a layer above the saltwater. When wells on land are pumped too quickly, the boundary between freshwater and salty groundwater rises and moves toward land. Wells near the coast can begin pumping saltwater and become useless.

Land Subsidence: Sinking Ground

A drop in groundwater levels can cause the ground surface to sink. As water levels in the aquifer fall, the upper portion of soil and sediment become dry. As air replaces the water in the pore spaces, the support that the water provided is removed. The weight of the ground above the lowered water table causes the sediment to compact, and the ground subsides, or sinks. This causes foundations to crack and buildings to tilt. Land subsidence can also damage highways, bridges, water lines, and wells.

THE ROLE OF GROUNDWATER IN THE WATER CYCLE

Groundwater begins its journey through the water cycle as precipitation, usually as rain or snow, in the atmosphere. Once the precipitation falls, some of it infiltrates the ground. Water that continues to move downward is stored as groundwater.

Groundwater moves slowly by meandering through soils and rocks underground. It is responsible for dissolving underground rocks to form caves and sinkholes. As water continues to move downward, it sometimes meets low permeability layers that it cannot travel through. The water moves horizontally across these layers, eventually emerging from the ground as springs or flowing into lakes, streams, and the ocean. From these water bodies, water evaporates into the atmosphere and begins the water cycle again.

5

Water in Rivers, Lakes, and Streams

All the rivers run into the sea; yet the sea is not full; unto the place from whence the rivers come, thither they return again.
—*Ecclesiastes 1:7*

These words, which were written in the Old Testament by the author of Ecclesiastes most likely between the second and fourth centuries B.C., show that rivers have been an important part in the movement of water on Earth since ancient times. These words also give a glimpse of the importance of rivers in transporting water through the water cycle.

WATERSHEDS: DRAINING THE LAND

Scientists call any body of water flowing in a natural channel (or trough) a stream regardless of its size. In everyday language, a large stream is usually called a river. Just as culverts drain rainwater from parking lots, streams drain excess water from the landscape. This excess water is surface runoff. It is what remains when more rain falls than can be absorbed into Earth, evaporated, stored in puddles or lakes, or used by plants. Gravity moves water downhill. Running water flows into streams or rivers because these features are lower than the ground around them. Rivers and streams eventually carry water back to the ocean.

A watershed is all of the land that drains into a river system. A watershed is also called a drainage basin or catchment. The Mississippi River has the largest drainage basin in North America. It collects water from the Rocky Mountains in the west to the Appalachian Mountains in the east. The total land area that drains into the Mississippi River is 1.2 million square miles (3.2 million km^2). Water flows into the Mississippi River from 31 U.S. states and two Canadian provinces. About 611,000 cubic feet (17,300 m^3) of water flow through the river each second. Although this is an astounding amount, about 7.5 million cubic feet (212,400m^3) of water flows in the Amazon River in South America each second. This flow is the largest of any river in the world—more than ten times that of the Mississippi River. The drainage area for the Amazon River is about 2.2 million square miles (5.8 million km^2). A huge rain forest is included in this drainage area.

The flow in most rivers is variable. In rainy weather, the flow will be higher than in dry weather. Flows are also higher in the spring when snow melts. Flows tend to decrease in very hot weather when more water is lost through evaporation and transpiration. In addition to runoff from rainwater, groundwater flow also contributes flow to streams and rivers.

THE WORK OF RUNNING WATER

The flow of water through the water cycle shapes Earth's surface. Running water grinds away the bottom and sides of stream channels. This process is called **erosion**. As water flows, it dislodges particles and lifts them into the flowing water. Water carrying sand or gravel is abrasive like sandpaper and wears away the channel bottom and sides. Pebbles caught in swirling waters can drill potholes into the floor of the channel. The force of the running water carves channels into solid rock. The running water also dissolves minerals as it flows.

Water carries the sand, gravel, pebbles, mud, or even boulders it lifted from the channel downstream as its sediment load. The

Mississippi River Basin

Figure 5.1 The Mississippi River Basin is one of the largest drainage basins in the world. It spans 4.76 million square kilometers (1.83 million square miles), including tributaries (streams feeding larger bodies of water) from 31 U.S. states and two Canadian provinces.

dissolved load is the portion carried in solution. Most of this comes into the stream through groundwater. The suspended load is all the materials that are temporarily or permanently carried in the flow without settling. The particles that are too large and heavy to be suspended bounce, roll, and slide along the stream bottom. These make up the bed load and are important factors in the erosion process.

Whenever the flow of a river slows down, it begins to drop the sediment, rocks, and gravel that it carried. This process is called deposition. The larger, heavier particles drop out first as gravity pulls them down. The finer particles are able to stay suspended longer and settle out further downstream when the water flow slows down. For this reason, deposits are sorted by size. Gravel collects in one location and mud in another. Geologists use the term *alluvium* to describe the sediment deposited by a stream.

Streams cannot erode their channel deeper and deeper forever. They can only cut down to the depth where the mouth of the stream enters the ocean, a lake, or another stream.

SHAPING THE LAND
Valleys and Canyons

When the land is much higher than the mouth of the stream, erosion caused by water can create deep troughs in the land as the water travels to the sea. If the walls of the trough have a gentle slope, a valley is formed. If the walls have a steep slope, a canyon is formed. The Grand Canyon is one of the most famous examples of the work done by running water. About 17 million years ago, a huge block of Earth's crust rose higher than the surrounding land. This block of land, known as the Colorado Plateau, is roughly centered on the Four Corners region of the southwestern United States, which encompasses portions of Arizona, Utah, Colorado, and New Mexico. Streams that once flowed over fairly flat land responded to the rise by cutting deep channels in the high grounds. The Grand Canyon is the deepest of these channels. At its deepest point, the floor of the canyon is 6,000 feet (1830 m) below the ground.

Rapids and Waterfalls

A rapid is a portion of rough water along a river or stream. Rapids usually form where water flows over large rocks on the river bottom. Most rapids form when the slope of the river becomes steeper. They also form when the river quickly narrows. The chaotic flow creates a mixture of bubbles and air called whitewater.

When the slope of the river bottom becomes so steep that water free falls downstream over a cliff or ledge, it creates a waterfall. These ledges usually form when hard rock resists being eroded by the stream. Softer rock downstream erodes at a quicker rate. Water plunges over the ledge to a deeper stream channel below. Waterfalls seem to be permanent features of the landscape. Yet waterfalls will eventually disappear as erosion slowly eats away on the overhanging ledge, causing it to eventually collapse. Niagara Falls is a popular tourist attraction located along the Niagara River between the

Figure 5.2 The deep, water-carved channels of the Grand Canyon are typified in this view down the Colorado River in Marble Canyon.

twin cities of Niagara Falls, New York, and Niagara Falls, Ontario, Canada. Diverting some of the river flow to hydroelectric plants has slowed the rate that the waterfall cuts upstream.

Deltas

Deltas form when running water flows into a body of standing water, causing the flow to slow and sediment to settle. Deltas get their name from the Greek letter, delta, which is written as the symbol Δ. This name described the triangular-shaped delta formed by the Nile River. Many deltas do not take on the triangular shape. The delta formed by the Mississippi River is one example. New Orleans, Louisiana, now sits where an ocean existed 5,000 to 6,000 years ago. Over time, enough sediment settled out to form dry land. The New Orleans delta actually formed by several deltas joining together. As sediment settled from the water, the land built up, and the slope of the Mississippi River became too shallow. The river shifted its path in a different direction to follow a shorter and steeper path to the Gulf of Mexico. Each time the river's path shifted, a new delta area formed.

The Mississippi delta's path has shifted about every 1,000 years in the past. In the 1950s, engineers noticed that the river's path was beginning to shift westward to the Atchafalaya River. This would have created a new route to the Gulf of Mexico. Industry and developments along the Mississippi River depended on the river's current path. The U.S. Corps of Engineers constructed the Old River Control Structure to prevent the river from shifting. This structure includes large floodgates that open or close as needed to allow water to flow. The purpose of the structure is to maintain 70% of the flow to Lower Mississippi River and 30% of the flow to the Atchafalaya River channels.

Meandering Streams

A boat traveling down the Mississippi River could not follow a straight path. The river channel winds back and forth in snakelike bends called **meanders**. In fact, if traveling from Memphis to New Orleans, a boat would cruise more than 600 miles (966 km) to travel what would be 350 miles (563 km) if done in a straight line. Meanders develop in areas where the river has a gentle slope. Even if a stream starts out straight, it has the tendency to develop into a meandering stream. Fast-flowing water erodes the sides of streams, cutting out more of a stream's outer curve. Each curve begins to

Figure 5.3 American Falls, one of three waterfalls that make up Niagara Falls, has a 188 feet (57 m) drop.

bend outward more. On the inside edge of curves, the water slows down, depositing the sediment that it eroded. A wedge-shaped deposit that forms is called a point bar.

As erosion continues, the neck of land between two meanders narrows. The river eventually erodes through the narrow neck of land, joining the next bend. An oxbow lake forms when the original meander is cut off from the rest of the river, forming a crescent-shaped body of water.

FLOODS: RAGING WATERS

Floods occur when the flow of water in a river is so great that the channel cannot hold it and the banks overflow. Floods are part of a stream's natural behavior. Yet, they are damaging and deadly, often

Formation of Meanders, Point Bars, and Oxbow lakes

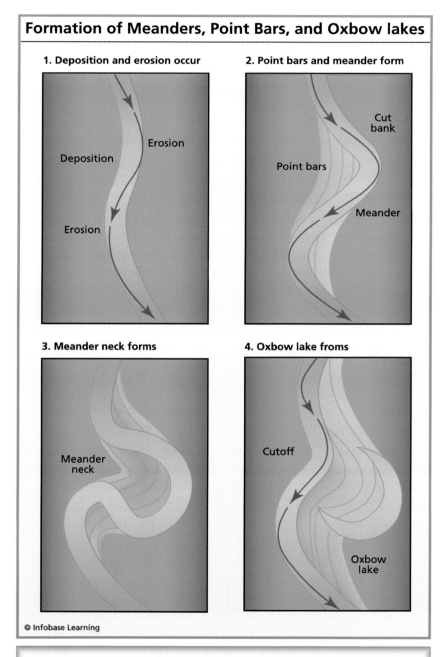

1. Deposition and erosion occur

Erosion

Deposition

Erosion

2. Point bars and meander form

Cut bank

Point bars

Meander

3. Meander neck forms

Meander neck

4. Oxbow lake froms

Cutoff

Oxbow lake

© Infobase Learning

Figure 5.4 Meanders form because erosion occurs faster on the outer bank of a curve, and deposition takes place on the inner curve. Over time, a stream that is cutoff will form an oxbow lake.

washing away crops and buildings while filling cities with water. The land bordering rivers and streams is normally dry but becomes covered with water during floods is the river's flood plain.

Seasonal floods gradually cover a large area with water. They take a few hours to several days to develop. Seasonal floods usually happen during a region's rainy season or in the spring when snow melts. On the other hand, flood waters rise extremely fast in a **flash flood**. These usually happen when rainfall is heavy or after a dam collapses. Mountain areas are at risk for flash floods because steep slopes act as funnels to send runoff into canyons. Development in urban areas increases the likelihood of flash floods because very little water can soak into roofs, streets, and parking lots. Instead, the water drains off these surfaces very quickly. Another cause of flash floods is the rise of water in frozen rivers. As the water level gets higher, the ice breaks up. As the ice flows downstream, it causes an ice jam that clogs the river. Water builds up behind it just as it would behind a man-made dam. When the ice dam breaks, the water gushes downstream.

When rivers flood, the sediment carried in their waters is deposited along the edge of the channel. Over time, the sediment builds up forming ridges on each side of the stream called natural levees.

FLOOD CONTROL

Structures are often built to lessen the destruction that floods cause. *Artificial levees* are earthen mounds that are built on the banks of rivers to control flooding. These levees create more water storage in the channel. Sometimes artificial levees are made of concrete. One problem with levees is that they may not survive the most extreme, but rare, flooding events. When these levees fail, they often prevent the flood waters from draining back into the channel as they recede.

Flood-control dams are built to store excess runoff, thus reducing flooding downstream. Although the stored water must eventually flow downstream, the dams can release it slowly after river levels have fallen. One drawback of dams is that they trap sediment and thereby block it from flowing downstream. This process allows deltas and flood plains to erode.

Case Study:
Big Thompson Canyon Flash Flood

Saturday, July 31, 1976, was a typical sunny day in Big Thompson Canyon, located northwest of Denver, Colorado. It was the height of tourist season in Colorado. In addition, it was the eve of the hundredth anniversary of Colorado's statehood. Approximately 3,500 people headed to the mountain canyons to escape the heat and enjoy camping, hiking, and fishing. Little did they know that disaster was brewing in the atmosphere.

Big Thompson River begins high in the Rocky Mountains near Estes Park, Colorado. The river drops almost half a mile (0.8 km) from top to bottom. Canyon walls are steep and rocky and jut straight up in some places. U.S. Highway 34 runs through the canyon.

At about 6:30 P.M. thunderstorms began to form. The thunderstorms stalled for more than 3 hours over the Big Thompson Canyon, dumping 12 to 14 inches (30 to 36 cm) of rain on the area. This amount of rainfall is almost equal to an entire year of rainfall for this area. It has been estimated that 7.5 inches (19 cm) of rain fell in about an hour. Water rushed down the canyon. People had only minutes to escape. Those who climbed to higher ground had the best chance of survival. Many who tried to flee through the canyon in their vehicles did not survive.

Rivers that were only a few feet deep grew to a depth of nearly 20 feet (6 m). The river flow was estimated at up to 25 feet per second (7.6 m per second). Cars and buildings were swept away. The roaring waters washed boulders down the canyon—even a boulder that weighed about 275 tons (250,000 kilograms). These boulders smashed everything in their path.

The Big Thompson Canyon flash flood destroyed 418 homes and 438 automobiles. Flooding caused over $35 million in damages (in 1976 dollars) and 145 deaths in Big Thompson Canyon.

One approach to flood control that does not require construction is creation of zoning restrictions for areas at high risk of flooding. Local land use policies often limit construction in areas that are prone to flooding. This reduces the amount of damage that floods

Flooding Caused by Hurricane Katrina in New Orleans

Tropical storm Katrina formed over the Bahamas on August 23, 2005. It strengthened to a Category 1 hurricane and crossed southern Florida on the evening of August 25, 2005. Sustained winds were 80 miles per hour (129 km per hour) at landfall but weakened as the hurricane crossed the tip of Florida. Upon entering the Gulf of Mexico, Katrina strengthened to a Category 5 storm and moved northward. It weakened and made landfall again as a Category 3 storm on the morning of August 29, 2005, just east of New Orleans, Louisiana. Damaging winds of 127 miles per hour (204 km/h) and record-breaking storm surges of 25 feet (7.6 m) in some places washed communities along the Gulf Coast right off the map.

The devastation of New Orleans happened hours after the eye of the hurricane passed. New Orleans lies between the Mississippi River on the south and Lake Pontchartrain on the north. The city sits 7 feet (2 m) below sea level, like a bowl in the ground. Artificial levees and flood walls were built around the city to protect it from flooding. As storm surges blew into Lake Pontchartrain, its level rose, pressing against the levees and flood walls. The high waters eventually broke through a weak area in a flood wall of the Industrial Canal. Other breaks followed.

As water filled the bowl-shaped landscape, it also filled some houses to their rooftops in minutes. Residents scrambled to attics and roofs as 80% of the city became submerged. The failure of New Orleans' hurricane protection system is one of the worst disasters in U.S. history.

can cause. These restrictions often require more appropriate uses for these areas, such as for a park, that could handle occasional flooding. Sometimes, building codes require structures to be elevated off the ground.

Figure 5.5 After the Hurricane Katrina passed over New Orleans on August 29, 2005, more than 50 breaches in drainage canal levees caused massive flooding. Within two days, 80% of the city was flooded.

LAKES

At first glance lakes may seem like isolated water bodies, but they are part of a larger system. Lakes receive water from precipitation, runoff from the surrounding watershed, and groundwater flow. Gases and particles from the atmosphere enter lakes through precipitation. Runoff carries dissolved materials, soil, leaves, and twigs into lakes. A lake's condition is therefore affected by the environment around it and by what is already in the lake.

Because water is constantly moving through the water cycle, water in lakes moves, too. Just as a bathtub overflows when it becomes too full, lakes overflow when more water than they can hold enters them. The overflow in most lakes leaves by way of a stream. Evaporation returns water in lakes to the atmosphere. Lakes also lose some of their water to groundwater.

The amount of time that it takes for the water volume of a lake to be "flushed" and replaced with new water is called the residence time. It is the volume of the lake divided by the outflow. In the water cycle, lakes serve as a storage reservoir. The residence time basically gives the average time that water remains in storage. Water residence times for the Great Lakes are 191 years for Lake Superior, 99 years for Lake Michigan, 22 years for Lake Huron, 6 years for Lake Ontario, and 2.6 years for Lake Erie.

Lakes and Temperature

Most liquids get denser as the temperature gets colder (more mass or weight per unit volume). As water cools, it becomes denser; it reaches its maximum density at 39.2°F (4°C). Water freezes at a lower temperature of 32°F (0°C); therefore, as water cools beyond 39.2°F (4°C) to the freezing point, the density actually increases. This process allows the solid ice, which is less dense and lighter than liquid water, to form on top of lakes. This phenomenon prevents ice from forming on the bottom of lakes, which would destroy fish habitat. Also, the layer of ice that forms on top of lakes helps to insulate the lake from further heat loss to the environment.

Swimmers in lakes in the summer might notice colder water near their feet (at the bottom of the lake) than that at the surface of the lake. This horizontal layering effect in lakes in which warm (less dense) surface water lies over cool (dense) bottom water is called stratification. Typically, the water separates into the following three regions:

- The epilimnion is the uppermost layer of a lake containing warmer water. Wind and surface waves contribute to this layer being well mixed.
- The hypolimnion is the unmixed layer of cold water at the bottom of a lake.
- The metalimnion is the layer of water between the epilimnion and hypolimnion where temperature and density change rapidly in the vertical direction.

When lakes are stratified, the water in the different layers does not mix unless it is forced to mix by boat passage, storms, or some other means. In the fall, air temperatures drop, and surface water temperatures begin to cool. As the water cools, it becomes denser and sinks, thus breaking through the stratified layers. As a result, the water within the lake is allowed to mix. This process is called lake turnover. In shallow lakes, turnover happens more frequently because strong winds, storms, and cold rain can cause mixing.

Trophic State

The nutrient enrichment of lakes is called eutrophication. It increases biological productivity. This means the numbers of plants and animals in the lake increase. Nutrients, such as nitrogen and phosphorus, cause plants to grow. However, input of too many nutrients can cause undesirable events in lakes. In order to discuss eutrophication in lakes, scientists have developed a classification of lakes based on their trophic state, or degree of eutrophication. Scientists find it hard to count the number of algae cells growing in a lake. Instead, they determine the trophic state of a lake by measuring the total chlorophyll, total phosphorus, total nitrogen, and water clarity. The definitions of words used to describe trophic states are better understood by breaking them down. The root word *trophic* means "relating to nutrition," the prefix *oligo* means "lacking," the prefix *meso* means "midrange," the prefix *eu* means "sufficient or good," and the prefix *hyper* means "over abundant." The four trophic state categories include the following:

- In oligotrophic lakes, the lack of nutrients causes few algae to grow. The water is clear and the lakes often have a sandy or gravel bottom. Oligotrophic lakes have the lowest level of biological productivity. Thus, these lakes have few plants, fish, or wildlife. Oxygen is available through the entire depth of the lake.
- In mesotrophic lakes, a moderate amount of nutrients allow these types of lakes to be moderately productive. The water is still somewhat clear but has a greenish color. The hypolimnion at the bottom of the lake may lack oxygen in the summer.
- Eutrophic lakes have high levels of nutrients and are very productive. The murky water supports much plant growth. Eutrophic lakes have the potential to support lots of fish and wildlife. They are often dominated by algae, and the hypolimnion lacks oxygen in summer.
- Hypereutrophic lakes have the highest level of nutrients and productivity. They lack clarity because the water is clouded with algae. Hypereutrophic lakes have abundant amounts of plants, fish, and other wildlife.

Nutrients are added to lakes through wastewater disposal, agriculture, and runoff from landscapes, golf courses, and shopping centers. Increased nutrients speed up the eutrophication of lakes. As lakes become more eutrophic, algae growth increases, and water clarity decreases. As nutrients increase, the growth of large plants also increases. Algae growth caused by increased nutrients increases the number of fish in a lake. In fact, fish farmers often add fertilizer to their ponds to increase the fish populations.

Lakes with shorter residence times, usually less than 10 days, have fewer problems with algae growth because algae are flushed out before they can grow in the lake.

Oxygen in Lakes

Fish and other aquatic organisms require oxygen to live. This oxygen cannot come directly from the oxygen that makes up water (H_2O) because this oxygen is bound to two hydrogen atoms. Instead, aquatic organisms depend on dissolved oxygen gas (O_2) that enters water from plants and the atmosphere. Plants produce oxygen by a process called photosynthesis in which carbon dioxide, water, and the energy from sunlight are used for plant growth. Oxygen is released as a waste product. Oxygen from the atmosphere enters water by a process called diffusion. This occurs because the concentration of oxygen in the air is greater than that in the water, allowing oxygen in the air to dissolve into the surface of the water. Wind creates waves, which provides more surface area for the diffusion of oxygen to occur. Often man-made aerators are installed in lakes to add more oxygen to the water.

Fish kills often result if oxygen levels in a lake become too low. Fish kills sometimes occur after large numbers of plants and algae die, such as after herbicides or algaecides are added to a lake. It is also experienced after large storm events wash great amounts of organic matter like leaves and twigs into the water. Animal wastes from pastures or human wastes from septic tanks also get washed into lakes. Bacteria in lakes use oxygen in the water to break down, or decompose, the waste and debris. If too much oxygen is used up, there is not enough oxygen remaining to support fish life, and they die.

6

Water in Oceans and Ice

E arth has five oceans: the Pacific, Atlantic, Indian, Arctic, and Southern Oceans. All of the oceans are connected into one global ocean. In fact, Earth is sometimes called the "blue planet" or "blue marble" because oceans cover over 70% of its surface. Oceans play an important role in the water cycle. According to the National Aeronautics and Space Administration (NASA), 78% of precipitation worldwide falls over the ocean. Additionally, oceans are the source of 86% of evaporation globally. An estimated 96.5% of the water on Earth occurs in the oceans and seas as salty water.

CURRENTS: RIVERS IN THE OCEAN

Water in the ocean does not stand still. Instead, it flows similar to water in rivers. Well-defined streams of moving water in the ocean are called **currents**. These currents move at two levels: surface currents and deep currents.

Winds drive surface currents. As air blows across the ocean's surface, it drags the water with it. Because Earth spins, air that would normally move between the equator and the poles gets turned aside, causing surface currents north of the equator to move toward the right. South of the equator, surface currents move toward the left.

Figure 6.1   This image of Earth image was taken by the GOES 8 weather satellite, one of many weather satellites designed and built by NASA but operated by the National Oceanic and Atmospheric Administration. Since GOES 8 retired in 2003, other GOES satellites have replaced it. These satellites have become indispensable for imaging clouds and measuring cloud heights and information scientists need for three-dimensional weather models.

Sinking and rising water causes deep currents. Dense seawater sinks below less dense seawater. This rising (upwelling) and sinking (downwelling) caused by density differences moves seawater around the globe in a pattern called the **global conveyor belt**. The global conveyor belt is also called **thermohaline circulation** because temperature (*thermo*) and salinity, or saltiness (*haline*), affect the density of seawater.

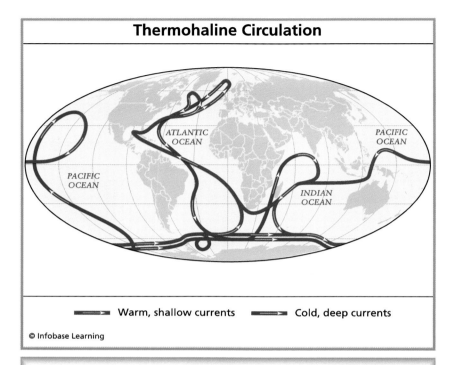

Thermohaline Circulation

Warm, shallow currents   Cold, deep currents

© Infobase Learning

Figure 6.2   The constant motion of the world's oceans is driven by thermohaline circulation, also called the global conveyor belt.

When sea ice forms in the polar regions, salt does not freeze. It is left behind causing seawater to become saltier and thus denser. The denser water sinks, and surface water is pulled in to replace it. This water becomes cold, saltier, and dense enough to sink. This process begins deep ocean currents that move the global conveyor belt.

Moving water carries the Sun's heat around Earth. The Gulf Stream carries heat from the tropics into the North Atlantic. Here the heat releases to the atmosphere, which helps to warm the region. Hurricanes often follow the Gulf Stream because heat is available to maintain the storms.

Ocean temperatures affect evaporation. Warm ocean currents that flow by continents allow more evaporation, thus increasing rainfall. Cold ocean currents allow less evaporation, resulting in dryer areas.

El Niño

Off the west coast of South America, an event called **El Niño** takes place. It is caused by an upset in the balance between winds and currents in the tropical Pacific Ocean. Normally, the western Pacific Ocean off the coast of Indonesia is warm, which causes low air pressure and heavy rainfall. Eastern Pacific waters off South America are usually cooler with less rainfall and higher air pressures. These pressure patterns drive winds from South America westward towards Indonesia. These winds confine the warm waters to the western Pacific Ocean.

In El Niño events, the system balance breaks down. Westward blowing winds weaken, or they even reverse direction and blow eastward. This weakening or reversal in direction allows the warm water off the Indonesian coast to move toward South America, bringing thunderstorms and rainfall. The warm water from Indonesia mixes with the cold water off South America and the temperatures balance out. Changes in this region trigger changes in weather worldwide. Although some have called El Niño an abnormal event, it occurs about every 3 to 6 years.

The 1997–1998 El Niño was the strongest ever recorded. Its effects were felt worldwide. It caused drought in Australia, forest fires in Indonesia, and severe hurricanes and typhoons in the Pacific. The Caribbean had a milder hurricane season than usual. In the United States, California received double the normal precipitation during the winter rainy season. Floods and mudslides claimed several lives and damaged properties. The southern United States also experienced above normal rainfall, and Florida experienced numerous tornadoes.

El Niño, which means "the Boy Child" in Spanish, was named by South American fishermen. The name refers to the Christ Child because El Niño occurs most often around Christmas.

RESTLESS SEAS

Tides

Tides are the daily rise and fall of sea levels at a point on Earth. Tides are visible ocean movements observed since ancient times. Not until Sir Isaac Newton (1643–1727) developed the laws of gravitation in the seventeenth century did people begin to understand tides. Newton showed that there is an attraction between two bodies. As the bodies get farther apart, the attraction decreases. Thus, the gravitational pull of the Sun and Moon on Earth causes tides.

On the side of Earth that is closest to the Moon, the Moon's pull causes oceans to deform and bulge outward. Because gravity decreases as two bodies get farther apart, the pull of the Moon's gravity on the opposite side of Earth is less because it is farther away. This phenomenon causes oceans to have a second bulge on the opposite side of Earth from the Moon. As Earth spins once a day, it passes under the two bulges where water is pulled away from Earth. These are the two daily high tides. The two low tides occur in between the two high tide bulges.

The Sun affects tides less than the Moon does. At times when Earth, the Moon, and the Sun are in line with one another, gravitational pulls on Earth from the Moon and Sun are added together, thus causing the highest high tides and lowest low tides. These tides are called spring tides, and they occur twice a month. They are not named after the season but instead for the German word *springen*, which means "to leap up."

Waves

Waves are a common sight to anyone visiting the beach. As the breeze blows, the water surface begins to ripple. As the speed of the wind increases, ripples grow into waves. Stronger winds produce larger waves. Wave height increases when the following occurs:

- wind speed increases
- wind blows for a longer time
- wind blows the water over a longer distance

Watching a wave travel across the ocean surface gives the impression that large amounts of water travel in the wave. A cork

Tidal Bulges

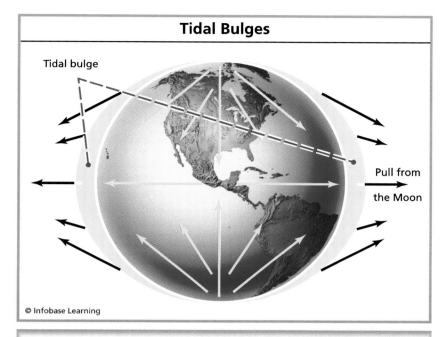

Tidal bulge

Pull from

the Moon

© Infobase Learning

Figure 6.3   Lunar gravity reduces the magnitude of terrestrial activity. Because Earth is rotating, this increases the tendency of every part of the planet to continue moving in a straight line and fly off into space. The result is two bulges, produced where terrestrial and lunar gravity pull in opposite directions. One bulge is directly beneath the Moon, and the other is on the opposite side of Earth.

dropped on the surface of the ocean, however, bobs up and down. It does not move along with the wave. Waves are simply energy traveling through water. The energy in waves crashing on the shore often comes from a storm far out at sea. Even waves created by tossing a pebble in a pond or splashing in a pool are visible evidence of energy traveling through the water.

HURRICANES: THE OCEAN'S SUPERSTORMS

On an evening in 1743, Benjamin Franklin (1706–1790) planned to study an eclipse of the Moon (lunar eclipse). However, he was not able to see the eclipse because Philadelphia, Pennsylvania, experienced a storm. He was surprised to hear that his brother had seen the eclipse in Boston, Massachusetts, because the storm did not begin until later. Franklin proposed that storms actually move, an idea that was not obvious in his day.

In 1821, William Redfield (1789–1857) documented a large storm in Connecticut. He noticed that trees that were blown down pointed to the northwest. Miles away, Redfield noted that trees had blown down in the southeastern direction. Based on these observations, Redfield concluded that the storm took the form of a great whirlwind. Thus, Redfield was responsible for making a groundbreaking discovery toward the understanding of hurricanes.

Hurricanes are intense storms over the North Atlantic Ocean, the Caribbean Sea, the Gulf of Mexico, and the northeastern Pacific Ocean. In other parts of the world, they are known by different names. In the northwestern Pacific Ocean, they are called typhoons. Near Australia and in the Indian Ocean, they are known as cyclones. Internationally, any hurricane-type storm is called a tropical cyclone.

Hurricanes are powerful, circular storms. The winds of a hurricane swirl around a calm center called the eye. The strongest winds in a hurricane are found in the eyewall, a band of rapidly rotating rings of thunderstorms outside the eye. In the Northern Hemisphere, Earth's rotation causes the winds to swirl in a counterclockwise direction. In the Southern Hemisphere, winds swirl in a clockwise direction.

Hurricanes begin over warm ocean water near the equator. The ocean water must be at least 80°F (26.5°C) for hurricanes to form. Warm water evaporates into the air. Moist air rises, lowering the air pressure beneath. As the rising air cools, it condenses and forms clouds, which grow into thunderstorms. The low-pressure area acts like a vacuum, funneling more moisture into the storm's center and fueling more thunderstorms. Moist air rises, pressure drops, and the cycle continues. The storm is called a tropical depression if winds are less than 39 miles per hour (63 kilometers per hour). When sustained winds reach 39 miles per hour (63 km/h), the system becomes a tropical storm and is given a name. At 74 mph (119 km/h), a hurricane has formed.

Figure 6.4   This satellite image shows the formation of Hurricane Katrina in 2005.

Hurricane Severity: The Saffir-Simpson Hurricane Wind Scale

The Saffir-Simpson Hurricane Wind Scale measures the damage potential of a hurricane. Wind engineer Herb Saffir and meteorologist

Bob Simpson developed the scale, which has been in use since 1972. It rates a hurricane from Category 1 (the weakest) to Category 5 (the strongest) based on its intensity at the time. A hurricane's maximum sustained surface wind speed is the determining factor in the category rating. It is the peak 1-minute wind measured at an elevation of 33 feet (10 m). The scale does not incorporate other hurricane-related damage, such as storm surge, flooding, or tornadoes. Previous versions of the scale, called the Saffir-Simpson Hurricane Scale, incorporate central pressure and storm surge into the category components. The following categories apply:

- Category 1 hurricanes have sustained winds of 74 to 95 mph (119 to 153 km/h). These storms can damage unanchored mobile homes, unprotected windows, roofing, swimming pool enclosures, signs, fences, and canopies. Large tree branches can snap.
- Category 2 hurricanes have sustained winds of 96 to 110 mph (154 to 177 km/h). These storms have a high probability of destroying older mobile homes built before 1994. Newer mobile homes could be destroyed as well. Structures may suffer major roof and siding damage, and entire roofs may be removed in poorly constructed homes. The destruction of swimming pool enclosures is common. Signs, fences, and canopies will be damaged. Snapped or uprooted trees will block roads. Power loss is expected.
- Category 3 hurricanes have sustained winds of 111 to 130 mph (178 to 209 km/h). These storms pose a high risk of injury or death to people and animals. Almost all older mobile homes will be destroyed. New mobile homes may have roof failure and wall collapse. Structures will experience a high percentage of roof and siding damage. Windows may be blown out of buildings. Most signs, fences, and canopies will be destroyed. Numerous roads will be blocked by trees. Electricity and water may be out of service for a number of weeks after the storm passes.
- Category 4 hurricanes have sustained winds of 131 to 155 mph (210 to 249 km/h). These storms pose a very high risk of injury or death to people and animals. Nearly all old and a high percentage of newer mobile homes will

be destroyed. Poorly constructed homes can completely collapse. Well-built homes can lose their roofs and possibly their exterior walls. Flying debris will damage unprotected windows and some protected windows. Almost all signs, fences, and canopies will be destroyed. Most trees and power poles will be downed, isolating residential areas. Power outages could last for months. Long-term water shortages will occur. Most of the area may be uninhabitable for months.

- Category 5 hurricanes have sustained winds greater than 155 mph (249 km/h). These storms pose a very high risk of injury or death to people and animals. Almost all mobile homes will be completely destroyed. Many frame homes will be destroyed, experiencing roof loss and wall collapse. Flying debris will damage almost all unprotected windows and many protected windows. Many buildings will experience complete collapse. Almost all signs, fences, and canopies will be destroyed. Most trees and power poles will be downed, isolating residential areas. Power outages could last for months. Long-term water shortages will occur. Most of the area may be uninhabitable for months.

HURRICANE NAMES

A storm is assigned a name once it reaches tropical-storm strength. Before this practice, hurricanes were identified by their latitude and longitude, which was confusing when more than one storm was in the same ocean.

During World War II, names corresponding to radio code words for each letter of the alphabet were used, such as Abel, Baker, and Charlie. From 1953–1977, female names were used in alphabetical order with each season's first storm beginning with the letter "A." Hurricanes were alternately assigned male and female names in the eastern Pacific in 1978 and in the North Atlantic in 1979. Names beginning with the letters Q, U, X, Y, and Z are not included in the list.

Once a storm becomes infamous for causing significant damage, its name is retired. Some retired hurricane names include Agnes,

Andrew, Camille, Charley, Gloria, Hugo, Ivan, Katrina, Mitch, Opal, and Wilma.

GLACIERS

Glaciers are masses of ice on land that move very slowly and last all year. Glaciers now cover about 10% of Earth's land surface. Although glaciers contain less than 2% of the world's total supply of water (saltwater and freshwater combined), they store over 68% of the freshwater as ice. Thus, this frozen fresh water is not available for human use.

Glaciers form from snow in areas that receive more snowfall in the winter than what melts in the summer. Snow changes into glacier ice very slowly. As new snow buries older snow, packing occurs. The snow recrystallizes and forms glacial ice. Up to one-fifth of the glacier is made of air trapped in bubbles. This glacial ice has a blue color.

Some glaciers are sheets of ice spreading over thousands of square miles of land. These glaciers are called ice sheets or continental glaciers. Today, there are only two continental glaciers; they are located in Greenland and Antarctica (the South Pole). The ice at the North Pole does not rest on land. Rather, it floats on water and is therefore not a glacier. Greenland's ice sheet covers 80% of the island or 700,000 square miles (1.7 million km^2). Antarctica's ice sheet covers almost the entire continent, a massive area of 5.3 million square miles (13.6 million km^2).

Mountain glaciers, or alpine glaciers, exist in mountain areas. Their shapes are determined by the shape of the mountains. Valley glaciers flow from high areas to low areas, usually following valleys that once held streams. When these glaciers flow out of the valley and spread into a broad sheet, they are called piedmont glaciers. Bowl-shaped glaciers are called cirques. Ice caps are another type of glacier; they completely bury the peaks and ridges of mountain ranges.

MOVING GLACIERS

The movement of glacial ice is called flow, even though ice is solid. One way in which the glaciers move is when the entire mass of ice

Figure 6.5   Malaspina Glacier in southeastern Alaska is considered the classic example of a piedmont glacier. Piedmont glaciers form when valley glaciers exit a mountain range onto broad lowlands, are no longer laterally confined, and spread to become wide lobes. Malaspina Glacier is actually a compound glacier, formed by the merger of several valley glaciers, the most prominent of which seen here are Agassiz Glacier (*left*) and Seward Glacier (*right*).

slips and slides on a layer of water from melted ice. Another way in which glaciers flow is by movement within the ice—when they change their internal shape without breaking apart. Unlike flow in streams, the flow in glaciers is seldom obvious. Some glaciers move so slowly that trees grow in the soils that collect on them. Others may move at a few feet or meters per day.

Glaciers, like flowing groundwater and rivers, erode land as they move. There are two primary processes by which glaciers erode the land: plucking and abrasion. Plucking occurs when ice melts and runs into cracks in the rock beneath the glacier. The water freezes in the cold environment. Because freezing water expands, rocks pry loose. Sediment and rocks of all sizes form and are carried by the glacier.

As the ice, sediment, and rocks slide along, grinding and scraping of the landscape occurs. This is called abrasion. Large rock fragments carried on the bottom of a glacier gouge and rip the underlying ground surface as the glacier moves. The long grooves and scratches that form are called glacial striations. By studying the direction of the grooves, scientists can determine the path that glaciers traveled.

If the sediment in the glacier is fine, abrasion polishes and smoothes the surface below, like sandpaper. In the same way that sanding wood produces sawdust, abrasion of rocks produces crushed rock called rock flour. Water flowing from melted glaciers is milky in color when it contains rock flour.

Glaciers create several landforms. They are responsible for widening, deepening, and straightening mountain valleys into U-shaped

Glaciers and Changing Sea Levels

One of the most dramatic effects of the last ice age was the change in sea level that occurred because of the formation and melting of glaciers. Glaciers act as a storage reservoir during water's journey through the water cycle. During the ice age, glaciers covered almost three times more area than they cover now and, therefore, stored much more water than they do now.

The snow that forms glaciers begins as evaporated water from the oceans. Growth of the glaciers must have caused a worldwide drop in sea levels as the water in ocean storage transferred to glacial storage. Estimates suggest that sea levels may have dropped over 300 feet (91 m), which means that land that is now covered by oceans was dry during the ice age. During that time, the Atlantic coast of the United States was over 60 miles (97 km) east of New York City.

Where the English Channel sits today, France and England were joined by dry land. Alaska and Siberia were connected by a land bridge across the Bering Strait. Southeast Asia and the islands of Indonesia were also connected by dry land. These land connections provided routes for people and animals to migrate or travel into other regions.

valleys. When the valley is flooded by rising seawater, inlets to the ocean called fjords are created. Glaciers carve sharp-edged ridges in mountains called arêtes and pyramidlike peaks called horns.

As glaciers drop sediment called till, additional landscape features develop. Boulders that are deposited with the till are called erratics if they are different than the rock below. Erratics are thus named because they were carried in from another location. Moraines are layers or ridges of deposited till. Flowing glaciers shape deposited sediment into long hills called drumlins. Sediment can bury blocks of ice that break off the end of a glacier. When the ice melts, a hole called a kettle hole remains in the ground.

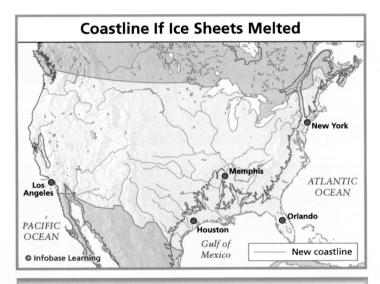

Figure 6.6   When glaciers melt, sea level rises. If the Greenland and Antarctic ice sheets melt, the resulting coastline would move inward—covering more land—from where it is now.

It has been suggested that if warmer temperatures caused all of Earth's glaciers to melt today, the sea level would rise 230 feet (70 m). Portions of the United States where people currently live would be covered by ocean.

ICE IN THE OCEAN

Large continental glaciers, or ice sheets, that flow into the ocean are called ice shelves. They are large, flat sheets of floating ice that remain attached to the land along at least one side. Antarctica's ice shelves cover 6 square miles (1.4 million km^2). Valley glaciers that flow into the ocean are called tidewater glaciers. They are called *ice tongues* if they extend far into the ocean.

Calving occurs when the front of a glacier breaks off. **Icebergs** form when blocks of ice calve off the front of glaciers after they have reached the ocean. About 80% to 90% of an iceberg lies below the ocean surface. The bottoms of large icebergs may reach hundreds of feet below the surface. The presence of icebergs in sea lanes is a threat to ships. In April 1912, the *Titanic* struck an iceberg and sank near Newfoundland, sending 1,503 passengers to a watery grave.

Not all floating ice comes from glaciers on land. Sea ice forms in polar regions, such as the Arctic Ocean, when the surface of the sea freezes in the polar climates.

PERMAFROST

Permafrost is permanently frozen ground that usually occurs in the polar areas. The ground stays cold enough that moisture in the soil and groundwater freeze. This underground water remains frozen all year except for the upper few feet.

Permafrost forms extremely strong foundations as long as it stays frozen. Heated buildings constructed on permafrost warm and melt the permafrost base, causing them to sink. To solve this problem, buildings in permafrost areas are placed on piles, or stilts. The ground remains frozen because cold air can circulate beneath the structure.

Wastewater Management

A fter businesses, residences, schools, hospitals, and industries use water, waste remains. This waste, called **wastewater** or sewage, is mostly liquid, but it contains small solid materials. The wastewater that a community produces must eventually go back into the environment. Before the wastewater is released, it must be treated to remove harmful substances. The goal of wastewater treatment is to protect public health and the environment.

THE NEED FOR WASTEWATER TREATMENT

Wastewater must be properly handled, or it will create undesirable conditions. If the wastewater collects and remains in one place, solid materials will decompose, or break down. As the solids breakdown, they produce foul-smelling gases. Bacteria from human intestines are released into wastewater through bathroom wastes. Contact with these untreated bacteria in wastewater can cause sickness and disease. In addition to bacteria, nutrients, such as nitrogen and phosphorus, found in the wastewater cause problems. Overgrowth of algae, weeds, and other plants in water bodies is a major problem with nutrients in wastewater. Because of these and other unfavorable qualities, wastewater must be removed from the places that create it.

Communities collect wastewater in underground pipes and send it to wastewater treatment plants, which are also called water reclamation facilities. A wastewater treatment plant uses a series of different processes to treat water. The purpose of each process is to remove and destroy harmful substances from the wastewater. Water leaving the wastewater treatment plant must be clean enough to safely return it to the environment or to use it for another purpose.

Scientists and engineers must determine what processes to include in wastewater treatment plants. They must first estimate how much water will flow through the plant each day to establish the size of the plant before construction. They also must know what substances are in the wastewater to determine what must be removed. Finally, they must know where the **effluent**, or treated water, leaving the plant will go. How the wastewater will be used determines how clean it must be.

TREATMENT METHODS

The first step in treating wastewater is called preliminary treatment. This step removes the large items that can clog pipes or damage equipment. Anything that can be flushed, including sticks, rags, rocks, bottles, toys, plastic, and trash, winds up in a wastewater treatment plant. These large items are caught on a screen as wastewater flows through the plant. Sand, gravel, and other small pieces that pass through the screen move into the grit chamber. The grit chamber is a large tank that slows down the wastewater, allowing the grit to settle to the bottom. Grit includes sand, gravel, and other small particles, such as egg shells, seeds, and coffee grounds, that will settle.

From the grit chamber, wastewater flows into sedimentation tanks for primary treatment. Physically removing solids that will float or settle takes place during primary treatment. Sedimentation tanks are large tanks that hold wastewater for several hours. Solids that were not heavy enough to fall out in the grit chamber settle to the bottom of sedimentation tanks. Materials that float, such as grease and oil, are skimmed off the top.

From the sedimentation tanks, wastewater flows on to the next stage of secondary treatment. Secondary treatment is the biological

Figure 7.1 Treatment structures at a wastewater treatment plant are shown.

removal of dissolved solids. Secondary treatment creates an environment that allows tiny organisms (sometimes called bugs by the wastewater operators) to feed on the waste. The temperature, oxygen levels, and time of contact are carefully controlled to encourage the organisms to eat the wastes dissolved in the water. The organisms naturally convert wastes that were dissolved into solids that settle out of the water. Carbon dioxide, cleaner water, and more tiny organisms are the end results of secondary treatment. Two common types of secondary treatment processes are activated sludge processes and trickling filters.

Tertiary treatment, or advanced treatment, improves the water quality enough to enter a water body, such as a river or ocean, or to be used in another beneficial way. This step removes additional suspended solids. Nutrients such as phosphorus and nitrogen may also be removed in this step. These are nutrients found in fertilizer that dramatically increase plant growth in water bodies. The plants can use up so much dissolved oxygen from the water body that there is not enough for the fish and other aquatic life to survive.

DEVELOPMENT MODIFIES THE WATER CYCLE

The traditional view of the water cycle has included water movement between the oceans, surface waters and streams, groundwater, and the atmosphere. Humans and our development of the land have changed the water cycle. Water is now withdrawn from rivers and groundwater reservoirs to supply drinking water and industrial and agricultural irrigation needs. As a result, less water flows in the rivers, and groundwater levels are declining in different areas. Construction of roads, parking lots, and buildings causes more runoff to flow into streams and rivers. This runoff is often routed from another area where it previously recharged groundwater. Additionally, runoff picks up pollutants—impurities, or waste materials, that lower the water quality—as they flow over land, carrying them into streams. As a result of these pollutants, the water quality of the receiving streams and rivers declines.

Growth in many communities has created a need for more water than what is currently available. Droughts worsen the water shortages. The pollution of existing groundwater and surface water supplies makes existing water unusable. In these communities, the wastewater that is collected cannot be considered a waste that can be released. Instead, the treated wastewater becomes a water resource. It must be reused to supply the community's water needs. The term *wastewater reuse* simply means using treated wastewater, or **reclaimed water**, for another beneficial purpose.

As water shortages become more common, scientists have found ways to assist the movement of water through the water cycle. Water reclamation and reuse can be an important subcycle of the water cycle. The use of reclaimed water, instead of freshwater, in many applications can help conserve existing water resources.

AGRICULTURAL AND LANDSCAPE IRRIGATION

The largest use of reclaimed water is for agricultural irrigation, for example, watering crops and pastures and irrigating commercial nurseries. The second largest use of reclaimed water is for landscape irrigation. Parks, playgrounds, athletic fields, golf courses, highway medians, flower beds, cemeteries, and residential lawns can all be watered with reclaimed water.

The estimated total cropland area in the United States and Puerto Rico in 1998 was 431 million acres (174 million hectares). Of this total amount, 55 million acres (22 million hectares) were irrigated. Worldwide, it is estimated that irrigation makes up 75% of the total water usage. Use of reclaimed water for agricultural irrigation has the potential to conserve tremendous amounts of freshwater.

The need for irrigation varies with the amount of rainfall received. In wet seasons, less watering is necessary. Irrigation amounts also vary with temperature. In hot weather when evaporation rates are high, more irrigation is needed for plants.

When using reclaimed water for irrigation of crops, the water content must be closely monitored. Some reclaimed water contains high amounts of salt that can damage plants. In addition, high amounts of solids in the reclaimed water can clog the irrigation system. On the other hand, the nitrogen contained in reclaimed water is beneficial because it reduces the amount of fertilizers that must be applied.

INDUSTRIAL REUSE

After irrigation, the next most common use of reclaimed water is in industrial processes. Although irrigation use is often seasonal, industries use fairly constant amounts of water all year long. Cooling water is the leading use of reclaimed water in industries; reclaimed water is used in cooling ponds or cooling towers of industries. Reclaimed water can also be used in other industrial processes, such as pulp and paper production, oil refineries, and textile processes.

Often the cost of using reclaimed water is too great for industries. Because the reclaimed water provided often needs additional treatment to meet specific water quality requirements, industries often must provide pretreatment at their facilities before they can use the water. Even the cost of constructing pipelines to bring the reclaimed water to the industrial facilities is often cost prohibitive.

A geothermal power plant in Santa Rosa, California uses reclaimed water in a unique way. Most power plants use a boiler to generate steam to produce power. The geothermal power plant in Santa Rosa injects reclaimed water mixed with groundwater into a geyser to produce the steam needed for its power generation.

GROUNDWATER RECHARGE

Another use of reclaimed water is to recharge groundwater. Reclaimed water can be pumped from wastewater treatment plants into surface spreading basins, which are also called percolation ponds or rapid infiltration basins (RIBs). These dry ponds often cover several acres. The reclaimed water is allowed to seep through the bottoms of the ponds into the ground to recharge the aquifer. This technique takes advantage of the natural filtering and cleansing ability of soils. Ponds cannot be filled continuously. The filling of a pond must be rotated to allow reclaimed water time to seep into the ground. For example, ponds may be filled for seven days, drained for seven days, and then allowed to dry for an additional seven days. While these are drying, other ponds are being filled.

Alternately, the water can be injected, or pumped through wells, directly into the aquifer. In coastal areas, drinking-water wells often draw in saltwater from beneath the coast. When this problem occurs, reclaimed water is pumped into the ground where it acts as a barrier to the flow of saltwater into wells.

Orange County, California began operating a groundwater replenishment system (GWR) in January 2008. Located between Los Angeles County and San Diego County, the Orange County Water District serves about 2.3 million people. Population and water demand were both predicted to increase at least 20% by 2020. Wells were drawing saltwater from the Pacific Ocean into the aquifer. At a grand total of $485 million, the GWR system takes highly treated wastewater and purifies it to meet drinking water standards. The reclaimed water is as pure as bottled water. The GWR system produces 70 million gallons per day (265 million liters per day) of treated water and generates enough pure water to serve 500,000 people. About half of the water from the GWR system is injected into the aquifer as a seawater barrier. The remainder is pumped into spreading basins to seep through the ground to recharge the aquifer.

RECREATIONAL AND ENVIRONMENTAL USE

Reclaimed water is also used for recreational and environmental purposes. It fills natural lakes, man-made lakes, and golf course ponds. These serve both recreational and environmental purposes. Although birds and fish use these lakes and ponds, they are not usually created solely for wildlife. They also often serve the recreational purposes of boating and fishing. Swimming in water bodies filled with reclaimed water is allowed in some states, but it is not common.

Reclaimed water is added to increase flow in some streams to protect fish habitat. In fact, small streams may depend on reclaimed water to maintain flow during long, dry periods, thereby providing the recreational benefit of fishing.

Wetlands are marshy, wet areas. The U.S. Environmental Protection Agency (EPA) estimates that over the last 200 years about 50% of the wetlands in the United States have been destroyed. Wetlands provide homes for plants and animals. They filter water flowing through them and store water to prevent flooding. Reclaimed water is added to create new wetlands or to restore existing ones. As an added benefit, the wetlands provide an additional treatment step for the reclaimed water that flows through them.

The production of artificial snow that is used mainly for skiing and snowboarding is an additional recreational use of reclaimed water.

URBAN USES

There are a variety of uses for reclaimed water in urban areas, including the popular use of cooling water for air conditioners. Irvine Ranch

Water District in California has operated a reclaimed water cooling system since 2002. In addition, they use the reclaimed water for toilet flushing. In California, Marin County has commercial laundries and car washes. Altamonte Springs, Florida, has 75 fire hydrants connected to its reclaimed water system, and the city cleans its streets with reclaimed water. Additionally, St. Petersburg, Florida has 308 hydrants connected to 290 miles (467 km) of reclaimed water pipes.

Water Conserv II: A Florida Case Study

Water Conserv II was the first reclaimed water project that the Florida Department of Environmental Protection permitted for the irrigation of crops eaten by humans. It is a joint reuse project for the city of Orlando, Florida, and Orange County.

Water Conserv II resulted from a court order to stop discharging effluent from the city and county wastewater plants into Shingle Creek. Studies determined that the best disposal option for the effluent was a combination of citrus irrigation and discharge to rapid infiltration basins (RIBs). Filters were installed to remove tiny solids in the reclaimed water to prevent clogging of the irrigation nozzles. High-level disinfection with chlorine was required to ensure that there were no detectable bacteria (fecal coliforms) or viruses. The facilities began operating in December 1986.

Reclaimed water is pumped from the city and county wastewater treatment plants approximately 15 miles (24 km) to the Water Conserv II Distribution Center. Four 5-million gallon (18.9 million liters) ground storage tanks store the reclaimed water. From the storage tanks, the water is pumped through a 24-mile (39-km) pipeline to the citrus groves. Up to 3,250 acres (1,315 hectares) of citrus is irrigated each year with this reclaimed water. When irrigation is not needed in wet weather or when there is more

POTABLE REUSE

Many communities use surface waters as the source of their drinking water supply. Some of these surface waters receive upstream inputs of reclaimed water. Use of these surface waters is considered an indirect potable (drinkable) reuse of reclaimed water. For direct potable reuse, the reclaimed water must be piped directly to a drinking

reclaimed water than is needed for irrigation, the water is sent to the RIBs. The RIBs consist of 1 to 5 cells (or ponds), each 350 feet (107 m) long by 150 feet (46 m) wide. The effluent drains through the sandy bottoms and then through the clay and limestone beneath the RIBs before recharging the Floridan Aquifer.

Since the project's startup, Water Conserv II has added irrigation of golf courses, nurseries, tree farms, and pasturelands. The permitted flow to the public access irrigation areas is 39 million gallons per day (147,600,000 L/d) and the permitted flow to the RIBs is 41 million gallons per day (155,200,000 L/d).

Some of the benefits of the Water Conserv II project include the following:

- Wastewater effluent discharge to environmentally sensitive surface water was eliminated.
- Preserves were established in the RIB areas for threatened and endangered plants and animals, such as the American alligator, gopher tortoise, great horned owl, and northern river otter.
- The withdrawal of irrigation water from the Floridan aquifer was eliminated.
- The reclaimed water from the RIBs recharges the Floridan aquifer. This recharge of reclaimed water helps to stabilize lake levels in the area.
- Citrus growers have seen faster young tree growth.
- Citrus growers have been able to eliminate the addition of some nutrients to their trees.

water treatment plant supply; it cannot be mixed with a surface water body.

Currently, there are no potable water reuse projects in the United States. For 150 days from 1956–1957, Chanute, Kansas, piped its reclaimed water to the drinking water treatment plant. The region was experiencing a five-year drought. The Neosho River, the city's water source, had dried up, leaving the city without water. Although the water had a pale yellow color and a musty odor and taste after treatment, it met the drinking water standards of the day.

Anytime reclaimed water is used in a drinking water supply, the key to its success is whether or not the public is willing to accept it.

Lake Elsinore Restoration

Dead fish. Dropping water levels. A lake covered in algae. Game fish overtaken by bottom-feeding carp and non-game threadfin shad. This dire scenario was Lake Elsinore in southern California.

The hot California sun evaporated Lake Elsinore, dropping the level of this 3,300-acre (1,335-ha) lake by 4.7 feet (1.4 m) per year. Dying algae used up the oxygen in the lake, causing fish to die. The nutrients released from the decomposing algae, along with warm temperatures and low lake levels, caused new algae growth. Lake Elsinore's future was in jeopardy.

The Lake Elsinore and San Jacinto Wastersheds Authority began plans to restore the lake. In five years, 1.3 million pounds (591,000 kg) of unwanted fish were captured in nets and removed. The lake was stocked with striped bass. A pipeline was built to deliver 4.5 million gallons (17 million L) of reclaimed water to the lake each day to replace water that had evaporated. Perforated (hole-filled) pipes were installed to bubble oxygen into the lake, and large mixing fans were placed in the lake to help circulate the oxygen through

ONSITE WASTEWATER SYSTEMS

In some areas (typically rural areas), wastewater systems are not available. The wastewater flowing from these homes and businesses must go into an onsite wastewater system. Commonly called septic systems, these onsite wastewater systems traditionally collect the wastewater in a buried septic tank. Solids settle to the bottom of the tank and bacteria break them down. Partially treated liquid waste flows out of a pipe near the top of the tank.

In a traditional septic system, liquid leaving the tank flows into a system of underground perforated pipes called a drain field or leach field. These pipes are underlain with gravel. Water seeps out of the

Figure 7.2   Private and public development surrounds the valley around Lake Elsinore in southern California.

the water. As a result of these efforts, Lake Elsinore is experiencing a comeback. Now a recreational destination for fishermen, the lake offers hybrid striped bass, largemouth bass, crappies, catfish, and carp.

pipes and travels through the gravel layer and into the soil. Additional treatment occurs through the natural filtering and cleansing ability of the soils as the water seeps downward.

According to the EPA, onsite wastewater systems serve about 25% of households in the United States. Septic system owners must maintain their systems so that they function properly and return safe water to the water cycle. Improperly functioning systems threaten public health and the environment because they cannot return clean water underground. Proper wastewater management practices use technology to aid Earth in moving water through the water cycle, just as it has been doing for millions of years.

Glossary

aqueducts   Channels that carry water

aquifer   Underground areas in soil and rocks that can store and transmit large amounts of water to supply wells and springs

atom   The smallest part of a chemical element that has the characteristics of the element; the building blocks of matter

Chinook wind   A warm, dry wind that blows down the eastern slope of the Rocky Mountains

clouds   Visible masses of tiny water drops or ice crystals suspended in the atmosphere

condensation   The change of state from a gas to a liquid

cooling process   Process that removes heat from the environment

currents   Well-defined streams of ocean water

Darcy's Law   The mathematical relationship of flow through a porous medium stating that the volume flowing through an area of material at a specified time depends on the permeability of the material and the hydraulic gradient

delta   Accumulation of sediment at the mouth of a river when running water slows upon entering standing water and drops the sediment that it was carrying

deposition   (1) The process of change from a gas directly to a solid without going through the liquid phase. (2) The process by which sediment settles out of flowing water

dew   Water that has condensed onto objects near the ground

dew point   The temperature to which air must be cooled for saturation to occur

Dust Bowl   A period of drought and severe dust storms in the 1930s resulting in agricultural and economic damage, particularly in the Great Plains region of the United States

El Niño   An extensive ocean warming beginning along the coast of Peru and Ecuador

erosion   The grinding away of soil and rock by moving water, ice, and air

effluent   Treated water that flows out of a wastewater treatment plant

evaporation   The change of state from a liquid to a gas

evapotranspiration   Sum of evaporation and plant transpiration

flash flood   A flood resulting from heavy rainfall or as a result of a dam break, causing floodwaters to rise very fast

flood   The overflow of water in a stream or river that occurs when the flow is so great that the channel cannot hold it

fog   A cloud resting at or very near the ground

freezing rain   Supercooled raindrops that freeze upon impact with the ground or another object

frost   Ice crystals that form on surfaces by deposition

geysers   Fountains of hot water and steam that erupt periodically from a vent in the ground

glaciers   Masses of ice on land that move very slowly and last all year

global conveyor belt   The rising and sinking of ocean water caused by differences in densities that correspond to differences in temperature and salinity; also called thermohaline circulation

groundwater   Water existing under the surface of Earth, below the water table, in cracks and pores of rocks or sediment

hydroelectric power   Electricity produced by flowing or falling water

hydrologic cycle   Continuous movement of water on, above, and under the surface of Earth; also called the water cycle.

iceberg   A large block of ice that breaks off the front of a glacier and falls into the sea

infiltration   Movement of water on the land surface into the soil

meanders   Snake-like bends in a stream channel

permeability   The ability of a material to allow water to pass through it

porosity   The percentage of open space in a material

precipitation   Liquid or solid water that falls from the atmosphere and reaches the ground

reclaimed water   Wastewater that has undergone treatment processes to meet the criteria for use in a beneficial way

relative humidity   A ratio of the amount of water vapor in the air compared to the amount required for saturation

runoff   The part of precipitation that flows across the ground surface and winds up in streams

saturation   The maximum amount of water vapor that the air can hold at a particular temperature and pressure

sinkholes   Circular holes in the land surface that form when underground caverns collapse

spring   Place where groundwater flows naturally to the ground surface

sublimation   The process of change from a solid directly to a gas without going through the liquid phase

supercooled water   Water below the freezing point that remains in liquid form

Thermals   Small column of rising, warm air created by uneven heating of the Earth's surface

thermohaline circulation   The rising and sinking of ocean water caused by differences in densities that correspond to differences in temperature and salinity; also called the global conveyor belt

tides   The daily rise and fall of sea levels at a point on Earth

transpiration   The release of water vapor from plants

topography   The shape and features of the Earth's surface

virga   Rain that evaporates before it reaches the ground

warming process   A process that releases heat into the environment

wastewater   Used water from homes, businesses, industries, and agriculture

wastewater reuse   The use of treated wastewater for another beneficial purpose

water budget   A tool scientists use to evaluate the availability of a water supply, utilizing the principle that the rate of change of water stored in an area is balanced by water flowing into and out of the area

water cycle   The continuous movement of water on, above, and under the surface of Earth; also called the hydrologic cycle.

water table   An underground boundary above which pore spaces in rocks and sediments contain mostly air, and below which they contain only water

water vapor   the gaseous form of water

wells   Holes dug or drilled into an aquifer to obtain water

Asano, Takashi. *Water Reuse: Issues, Technologies, and Applications*. New York, NY: McGraw-Hill, 2007.

Biswas, Asit K. *History of Hydrology*. Amsterdam: North-Holland Publishing Co., 1970.

Brutsaert, Wilfried. *Hydrology: An Introduction*. Cambridge, UK: Cambridge University Press, 2005.

Cech, Thomas V. *Principles of Water Resources: History, Development, Management, and Policy*. Hoboken, NJ: John Wiley & Sons, 2010.

Dooge, J.C.I. "The Development of Hydrological Concepts in Britain and Ireland Between 1674 and 1874." *Hydrological Sciences Bulletin* 19:3 (1974): 279–302.

Florida Lakewatch. *A Beginner's Guide to Water Management—Oxygen and Temperature*. Gainesville, FL: University of Florida Cooperative Extension Service, Institute of Food and Agricultural Sciences, EDIS, 2004. Available online at http://lakewatch.ifas.ufl.edu/circpdffolder/Circ109_OxygenTemp.pdf. Accessed February 4, 2011.

Gleick, P.H., "Water Resources," in *Encyclopedia of Climate and Weather*, Ed., S.H. Schneider, New York, NY: Oxford University Press, Vol. 2, pp. 817–823, 1996.

Graumann, A. *Hurricane Katrina: A Climatological Perspective*. Asheville, NC: U.S. Department of Commerce, National Oceanic and Atmospheric Administration, National Environmental Satellite Data and Information Service, National Climatic Data Center, 2006. Available online at http://purl.access.gpo.gov/GPO/LPS105585. Accessed February 4, 2011.

Grotzinger, John P. *Understanding Earth*. New York: W.H. Freeman, 2007.

Hager, W.H., and C. Gisonni. "Finding Darcy at Dijon," *Journal of Hydraulic Engineering* 128 (2002): 454–459.

Jarrett, Robert D., and John E. Costa. *1976 Big Thompson Flood, Colorado: Thirty Years Later*. Reston, VA: U.S. Department of the Interior,

U.S. Geological Survey, 2006. Available online at http://pubs.usgs.gov/fs/2006/3095/. Accessed February 4, 2011.

Lutgens, Frederick K., Edward J. Tarbuck, and Dennis Tasa. *The Atmosphere: An Introduction to Meteorology*. Upper Saddle River, NJ: Pearson Prentice Hall, 2010.

Lutgens, Frederick K., and Edward J. Tarbuck. *Essentials of Geology*. Upper Saddle River, N.J.: Pearson Prentice Hall, 2009.

Marshak, Stephen. *Essentials of Geology*. New York, NY: W.W. Norton and Company, 2009.

National Hurricane Center Saffir-Simpson Team. "The Saffir-Simpson Hurricane Wind Scale." Available on the National Weather Service National Hurricane Center Web site at http://www.nhc.noaa.gov/pdf/sshws.pdf. Accessed February 4, 2011.

"North American Drought: A Paleo Perspective." Available on the National Oceanic and Atmospheric Administration Web site at http://www.ncdc.noaa.gov/paleo/drought/. Accessed February 4, 2011.

Oliver, John E. and John J. Hidore. *Climatology: An Atmospheric Science*. Upper Saddle River, NJ: Prentice Hall, 2002.

Parkinson, C.L., A. Ward, and M.D. King. *Earth Science Reference Handbook: A Guide to NASA's Earth Science Program and Earth Observing Satellite Missions*. Washington, D.C., National Aeronautics and Space Administration, 2006.

Ramey, V. "Trophic States of Florida Lakes." Available on the University of Florida Plant Management in Florida Waters Web site at http://plants.ifas.ufl.edu/guide/thermstrat.html. Accessed February 4, 2011.

Strangeways, I. *Precipitation: Theory, Measurement, and Distribution*. Cambridge, UK: Cambridge University Press, 2007.

Tchobanoglous, George, Franklin L. Burton, and H. David Stensel. *Wastewater Engineering: Treatment and Reuse*. Boston: McGraw-Hill, 2003.

Williams, Jack. *The Weather Book*. New York: Vintage Books, 1992.

Windelspecht, Michael. *Groundbreaking Scientific Experiments, Inventions, and Discoveries of the 19th Century*. Westport, CT: Greenwood Press, 2003.

"Understanding and Defining Drought." Available on the National Drought Mitigation Center Web site at http://www.drought.unl.edu/whatis/concept.htm. Accessed February 4, 2011.

U.S. Environmental Protection Agency and National Risk Management Research Laboratory. *Guidelines for Water Reuse*. Washington, DC: U.S. Environmental Protection Agency, 2004.

Further Resources

Books

Barnhill, Kelly Regan. *Do You Know Where Your Water Has Been? The Disgusting Story Behind What You're Drinking.* Mankato, MN: Capstone Press, 2009.

Casper, Julie Kerr. *Water and Atmosphere: The Lifeblood of Natural Systems.* New York: Chelsea House Publishers, 2007.

Flynn, Claire E. *Water World: Earth's Water Cycle.* New York: PowerKids Press, 2009.

Karpelenia, Jenny. *The Water Cycle.* Reading Essentials in Science. Logan, IA: Perfection Learning, 2005.

Rice, W.B. *Inside the Water Cycle.* Minneapolis, MN: Compass Books, 2010.

Schueller, Gretel H. *Rivers, Lakes, and Oceans.* New York: Chelsea House Publishers, 2009.

Trueit, Trudi Strain. *Rain, Hail, and Snow.* Watts Library. New York: Franklin Watts, 2002.

———. *The Water Cycle.* Watts Library. New York: Franklin Watts, 2002.

Web Sites

U.S. Environmental Protection Agency: Water for Kids
http://water.epa.gov/learn/kids/waterkids/waterforkids.cfm
> *This site provides a list of U.S. Environmental Protection Agency links to water information. Several of the sites include games, activities, or puzzles.*

National Earth Science Teachers Association: Windows to the Universe—Water
http://www.windows2universe.org/Earth/Water/overview.html
> *This site discusses oceans, rivers, groundwater, ice, clouds, and the water cycle. Each topic can be viewed at the beginner, intermediate, or advanced levels.*

National Oceanic and Atmospheric Administration: Hydrologic Cycle
http://www.nwrfc.noaa.gov/info/water_cycle/hydrology.cgi
> *This site describes the processes of the water cycle (evaporation, condensation, precipitation, interception, infiltration, percolation, transpiration, runoff, and storage) and a discussion on the water budget for the United States.*

National Weather Service: Cloud Classification and Characteristics
http://www.crh.noaa.gov/lmk/?n=cloud_classification
> *This site provides information about high-, middle-, and low-level cloud types along with other interesting clouds. Cloud photos are included.*

U.S. Geological Survey: Science in Your Watershed
http://water.usgs.gov/wsc/glossary.html
> *This site features definitions of water-related terminology.*

U.S. Geological Survey: Water Science for Schools—The Water Cycle
http://ga.water.usgs.gov/edu/watercyclesummary.html
> *This site describes the components of the water cycle (water storage in oceans, evaporation, sublimation, evapotranspiration, water in the atmosphere, condensation, precipitation, water storage in ice and snow, snowmelt runoff to streams, surface runoff, stream flow, freshwater storage, infiltration, groundwater storage, groundwater discharge, and springs).*

University of Illinois at Urbana-Champaign Weather World 2010 Project: Clouds and Precipitation
http://ww2010.atmos.uiuc.edu/(Gh)/guides/mtr/cld/home.rxml
> *This site describes cloud types and precipitation and provides photographic examples. The meteorology guide on the Web site menu includes links to information about the hydrologic cycle.*

Picture Credits

Index

About the Author

Nikole Brooks Bethea is a professional engineer licensed in Florida, Georgia, and Alabama. She received her bachelor's and master's degrees in environmental engineering from the University of Florida. She has 15 years of engineering experience, including the design of municipal drinking water and wastewater systems, environmental permitting, and environmental site assessments. She lives in Marianna, Florida, with her husband and four sons.